CROSS-CURRICULAR TEACHING AND LEARNING IN THE SECONDARY SCHOOL

MATHEMATICS

Why is cross-curric... ...able in the mathematics classroom?

Why can pupils so... ...phs in mathematics but not in science?

What might mathe... ...rn from the performing arts?

Cross-curricular ap... ...ch to offer the modern mathematics classroom. They can help teachers t... ...atics as a growing, relevant discipline that is central to much of modern life... ...rs to make sense of what they are doing and why. New contexts, new technolo... ...ualifications all make this an exciting time to be a cross-curricular teacher of m...

But cross-curricular ap... ...t always straightforward. Skills do not always transfer easily from one subject a... ...r, and a number of important decisions have to be made. How should this typ... ...lanned, or assessed? How might it fit into the wider curriculum? Are all cross-cu... ...ities equally useful for learners? Does mathematics have something to share with... ...ther curriculum areas?

This book tackles these issues... ...n, combining educational theory and contemporary research with practical ideas and... ...ions. From the mathematics of molecular geometry, wind turbines and impact craters to mathematical haikus, Babylonian clay tablets and juggling, each chapter is packed with examples for use in the secondary classroom.

Key features include:

- discussion of key issues and debates
- case studies to show you how others have used cross-curricular approaches
- a wide range of examples and practical activities to help you develop your own practice
- example approaches for planning and assessment.

Part of the *Cross-Curricular Teaching and Learning in the Secondary School* series, this book is essential reading for all students on Initial Teacher Training courses and practising teachers looking to holistically introduce cross-curricular themes and practices into their mathematics teaching.

Robert Ward-Penny teaches on the Secondary PGCE Mathematics Course at the University of Warwick.

Cross-Curricular Teaching and Learning in . . .
Series Editor: Jonathan Savage (Manchester Metropolitan University, UK)

The *Cross-Curricular* series, published by Routledge, argues for a cross-curricular approach to teaching and learning in secondary schools. It provides a justification for cross-curricularity across the Key Stages, exploring a range of theoretical and practical issues through case studies drawn from innovative practices across a range of schools. The books demonstrate the powerful nature of change that can result when teachers allow a cross-curricular 'disposition' to inspire their pedagogy. Working from a premise that there is no curriculum development without teacher development, the series argues for a serious re-engagement with cross-curricularity within the work of the individual subject teacher, before moving on to consider collaborative approaches for curriculum design and implementation through external curriculum links.

Cross-curricular approaches to teaching and learning can result in a powerful, new model of subject-based teaching and learning in the high school. This series places the teacher and their pedagogy at the centre of this innovation. The responses that schools, departments or teachers make to government initiatives in this area may be sustainable only over the short term. For longer-term change to occur, models of cross-curricular teaching and learning need to become embedded within the pedagogies of individual teachers and, from there, to inform and perhaps redefine the subject cultures within which they work. These books explore how this type of change can be initiated and sustained by teachers willing to raise their heads above their 'subject' parapet and develop a broader perspective and vision for education in the twenty-first century.

Forthcoming titles in the series:

Cross-Curricular Teaching and Learning in the Secondary School . . . The Arts
Martin Fautley and Jonathan Savage

Cross-Curricular Teaching and Learning in the Secondary School . . . English
David Stevens

Cross-Curricular Teaching and Learning in the Secondary School . . . Foreign Languages
Gee Macrory, Cathy Brady and Sheila Anthony

Cross-Curricular Teaching and Learning in the Secondary School . . . Humanities
Richard Harris and Simon Harrison

Cross-Curricular Teaching and Learning in the Secondary School . . . Using ICT
Maurice Nyangon

Cross-Curricular Teaching and Learning in the Secondary School . . . Mathematics
Robert Ward-Penny

CROSS-CURRICULAR TEACHING AND LEARNING IN THE SECONDARY SCHOOL
···
MATHEMATICS

Robert Ward-Penny

Routledge
Taylor & Francis Group

LONDON AND NEW YORK

This first edition published 2011
by Routledge
2 Park Square, Milton Park, Abingdon, Oxon, OX14 4RN

Simultaneously published in the USA and Canada
by Routledge
270 Madison Avenue, New York, NY 10016

Routledge is an imprint of the Taylor & Francis Group, an informa business

© 2011 Robert Ward-Penny

Typeset in Bembo by
Saxon Graphics Ltd, Derby
Printed and bound in Great Britain by
TJ International Ltd, Padstow, Cornwall

British Library Cataloguing in Publication Data
A catalogue record for this book is available from the British Library

Library of Congress Cataloging-in-Publication Data
Ward-Penny, Robert, 1980–
Cross-curricular teaching and learning in secondary education-- mathematics / by Robert Ward-Penny. -- 1st ed.
p. cm.
Includes bibliographical references and index.
1. Mathematics--Study and teaching (Secondary)--United States. 2. Mathematics teachers--In-service training--United States. 3. Effective teaching--United States. I. Title.
QA13.W37 2011
510.71′273--dc22
2010024131

ISBN13: 978-0-415-57203-3 (hbk)
ISBN13: 978-0-415-57204-0 (pbk)
ISBN13: 978-0-203-83563-0 (ebk)

Contents

List of figures

Acknowledgements

Sincere thanks to all those friends and colleagues who have offered feedback, ideas and encouragement whilst making their way through various drafts of this book: Sarah Blyth, Ian Boote, Graham Charles, Isobel Chester, Jenni Ingram, Peter Johnston-Wilder, Sue Johnston-Wilder, Vicky Larner, Clare Lee, Christian Lockley, Jonathan Savage and Marian Ward-Penny.

Thanks are also due to all those who have helped to inspire and construct the case studies contained in this book: for the case study in Chapter 1, Jim Vinton and Sophie Fitzgerald of Farnham Heath School; for the case study in Chapter 3, Alex Hughes of Ninestiles School, Birmingham; for the case study in Chapter 4 and the use of Figure 4.2, Garry Redrup and Ashley Green; for the case study in Chapter 8, Nick McIvor and David Hall; and for the case study in Chapter 9, Peter Ransom. Details of the 'Maths Circus' discussed in Chapter 8 can be found online at www.davidhallworkshopsandshows.co.uk.

Special thanks to Peter Raedschelders for permission to use his art in Chapter 6. Further examples of Peter's artwork can be found online at http://home.scarlet.be/~praedsch/.

Abbreviations

2-D	Two-dimensional
3-D	Three-dimensional
A2-level	The second and final part of A-level study
A-level	Advanced level (consists of AS + A2-levels)
ASCII	American Standard Code for Information Interchange
AS-level	Advanced Subsidiary level
AST	Advanced Skills Teacher
ATM	Association of Teachers of Mathematics
Becta	British Educational Communications and Technology Agency
C Standards	Core professional standards for teachers
c.	Circa
CCTV	Closed circuit television
CLIL	Content and Language Integrated Learning
CSMS	Concepts in Secondary Mathematics and Science
CUREE	The Centre for the Use of Research and Evidence in Education
DfEE	Department for Education and Employment
DfES	Department for Education and Skills
EAL	English as an additional language
FSMQ	Free-standing mathematics qualifications
GCSE	General Certificate of School Education
GDP	Gross domestic product
GIMPS	Great Internet Mersenne Prime Search
GPS	Global positioning system
HDI	Human Development Index
ICT	Information and communication technologies
ISBN	International standard book number
KS	Key stage
MA	Mathematical Association
MDF	Medium-density fibreboard
MEI	Mathematics in Education and Industry

NCETM	National Centre for Excellence in Teaching Mathematics
Ofsted	Office for Standards in Education, Children's Services and Skills
PE	Physical education
PED	Price elasticity of demand
PGCE	Postgraduate Certificate in Education
PLTS	Personal, Learning and Thinking Skills
PSHCE	Personal, Social, Health and Citizenship Education
Q Standards	Standards required for Qualified Teacher Status
QCA	Qualifications and Curriculum Authority
QCDA	Qualifications and Curriculum Development Agency
RE	Religious education
STEM	Science, Technology, Engineering and Mathematics
VAK	Visual, auditory, kinaesthetic

The context for cross-curricular mathematics

Of all of the subjects in the school curriculum, mathematics is one of the most ubiquitous. Skills taught in mathematics lessons are often fundamental to other subjects, and pupils' progress in other curriculum areas frequently depends on them being fluent in basic mathematical procedures. Many lessons in other subjects can be enhanced and made more meaningful through the use of mathematical methods and ideas, and mathematical thinking and problem solving is a critical skill across the curriculum.

However, mathematics often functions as a 'chameleon discipline' (Johnston-Wilder and Lee 2010), fading away against the background of whichever curriculum area it is supporting. Consequently, pupils often leave school without a real awareness of the scale of the power and relevance that mathematics has in modern society, and will continue to have in the future. For many pupils this lack of awareness is coupled with a debilitating lack of experience and confidence in applying mathematics in out of school contexts. A cross-curricular approach to mathematics is therefore both urgent and exciting, offering both teachers and learners a chance to engage with the subject in a way that is both more authentic and more motivating.

The book has three interrelated aims: to justify the importance of a cross-curricular approach to teaching and learning mathematics; to provide a wide range of examples; and to explore both the potential and pitfalls of such an approach. In order to meet these aims it will consider a wide range of issues. Some of these will be largely theoretical, whilst others will be purely practical; however all of them will ask you to reflect on and challenge your own practice. You may find it useful to have some paper and a pen to hand as you read, in order to note down your own thoughts and ideas.

Key objectives

By the end of this chapter, you will have:

- Considered what 'cross-curricular' teaching and learning might involve, and how it might be recognised in the classroom

- Reflected on your own views about, and experiences of, cross-curricular teaching and learning in mathematics
- Reviewed some of the recent curriculum changes and new qualifications which contain significant cross-curricular elements

Why is cross-curricular teaching important?

It is undeniable that we live in interesting and turbulent times, and that this century poses a number of challenges which are both complex and controversial. The Millennium Project (2009) identifies 15 global challenges currently facing humanity, including the following:

- How can sustainable development be achieved for all while addressing climate change?
- How can everyone have sufficient clean water without conflict?
- How can population growth and resources be brought into balance?
- How can the threat of new and re-emerging diseases and immune micro-organisms be reduced?
- How can shared values and new security strategies reduce ethnic conflicts, terrorism and the use of weapons of mass destruction?
- How can growing energy demands be met safely and efficiently?

It is clear that each of these questions involves knowledge, skills and understandings from more than one school subject area. For example, the issues surrounding the sourcing and delivery of clean water involve concepts typically located in a host of subjects including geography, biology, chemistry, technology, politics and economics. Each of these questions also draws heavily on techniques, ideas and thinking skills that are found in mathematics. In fact, mathematics is a fundamental element here and elsewhere; it is present wherever there is a call for quantification, measurement, modelling or logical analysis, and in this way it underpins the use of each of the other subjects mentioned. It is impossible to imagine any kind of approach to answering these challenges that would not use mathematics in some form. However, it is just as challenging to think of a way that mathematics could solve any of these problems as a stand-alone subject.

If we are to future-proof our pupils' developing mathematical facility, there is a need for us to present mathematics in a wider context and promote joined-up thinking between mathematics and other curriculum subjects. It is not only the future which is making this demand; there has already been a shift in the employment market, and new technologies and globalisation trends require flexible mathematical thinking as much as procedural competence (Hoyles *et al.* 2010). Cross-curricular approaches to teaching mathematics offer a range of ways of enhancing pupils' mathematical learning so as to address these needs and concerns.

Different organisations are beginning to recognise the need to rethink the way that mathematics is presented and delivered in schools, and at the time of writing there have been a number of significant changes in mathematics qualifications and curricula that involve, either explicitly or implicitly, cross-curricular perspectives on mathematics. Many of these changes are exciting ones that offer a range of new opportunities – and new challenges – to mathematics teachers. However, each has its own perspective on what 'cross-curricular' mathematics might entail, and so it is important to start this chapter by considering what you, and others, might mean by 'cross-curricular'.

What does 'cross-curricular' mean?

The term 'cross-curricular' is widely used by schools and educational organisations, but it can be quite difficult to formally define. Although 'cross-curricular' has an obvious semantic meaning, genuine cross-curricular activity transcends this: you would be unlikely to claim that an English teacher asking their pupils to turn to page 76 would constitute a genuine cross-curricular use of mathematics! So what does 'cross-curricular' mean?

> ### Reflective task
>
> Think about the term 'cross-curricular' and note down what it means to you. How might you recognise a cross-curricular activity in the mathematics classroom? When you have finished, put your jottings to one side, then review them once you have completed reading this chapter.

One way of answering this question is to suggest that a cross-curricular approach can be recognised not simply through an overlap in content, but through associated changes in both the teacher's pedagogy and the pupils' learning experience. It is in this sense that Savage offers the following definition elsewhere in this series:

> A cross-curricular approach to teaching is characterised by sensitivity towards, and a synthesis of, knowledge, skills and understandings from various subject areas. These inform an enriched pedagogy which promotes an approach to learning which embraces and explores this wider sensitivity through various methods.
>
> (Savage 2011: 8–9)

This definition moves beyond the immediate meaning of 'cross-curricular' to describe an approach that is in some sense *interdisciplinary*, combining two or more different schools of thought to address a problem. Tasks that fully satisfy this principle tend to be steered primarily by the nature of the problem, requiring new skill sets at different stages and a degree of criticality, self-reflection, and even metacognition on the part of the learner.

Savage's definition also contains a significant challenge for the mathematics teacher, as it encourages us to move beyond simply using scenarios from other subjects as decontextualised illustrations. For example, when teaching the topic of ratio, a teacher might draw two gears on the board, one with 18 teeth and one with 6 teeth, and ask the class how many turns of the smaller gear would equal one turn of the larger gear. This is a valid link to another subject area, but so far no knowledge, skills or understandings

3

have crossed between subjects. The pupils merely have to extract the numbers and select an appropriate operation. To this end, the activity could be developed by introducing ideas from technology such as 'velocity ratio' and 'torque', or better still, by presenting pupils with a physically meaningful problem together with a set of gears that they could use to help devise and test a solution.

Another challenge arising from this definition is to separate off our understanding of 'cross-curricular activities' from the more prominent curriculum area of using and applying mathematics. Cross-curricular activity often uses skills of application and modelling, but in addition it is always informed (and often steered) by content and skills drawn from other subject areas. 'Using and applying' investigations, however, can sometimes be based around abstract mathematics, where enquiry can be steered purely by an interest in the structure and properties of mathematics itself.

Throughout this book you will find examples of many different types of cross-curricular activities, from using mathematics to investigate the effects of natural disasters to integrating performing arts techniques in order to explore the properties of quadrilaterals. Some of these examples could easily take place as a small part of a regular mathematics lesson, whereas others are more extensive, and might require extra resources or a wider level of school participation. In every case, what is important is that the blurring of subject boundaries impacts upon the pupils' experiences, the teacher's practice, or both. When these conditions are satisfied, activities can have a substantial impact, ideally developing pupils' understanding and motivating their study in each of the subject areas involved.

There are other ways in which 'cross-curricular' teaching and learning can be considered, and some of these will be touched upon in the discussion below. As you read through this book you will undoubtedly continue to develop your own understanding of the term 'cross-curricular', and the role of cross-curricular teaching within the mathematics classroom.

Why teach mathematics in a cross-curricular way?

Having established a working definition for what we mean by 'cross-curricular', the next step is to consider some of the different reasons why we might choose to teach mathematics in a cross-curricular way.

Authentic activity

Although many arguments can be made for the benefits of teaching mathematics in a cross-curricular way, the simplest, and perhaps most important, is that cross-curricular activities are more authentic. The vast majority of the actions that we perform as adults are cross-curricular, since they draw on a range of skills that have been traditionally taught separately in different curriculum subjects. When adults use mathematics, they often use it to provide one perspective on a problem that is then considered alongside many others.

For example, consider the following scenario. During his weekly shop, a father must decide whether to get three tins of Brand A (60 p for 500 g) or four tins of Brand B (45 p for 400 g). At first, this problem might seem like a purely mathematical one, as this problem can be 'solved' using proportional reasoning. Yet in reality, such a decision would be influenced by a number of other factors. Does his family have a preference for one brand or the other? Is one brand healthier than the other? When he cooks for his family, does he find a 500g tin too big, and so does he create waste? Is one brand a fair-trade product, produced in a more ethical way? None of these questions devalue the importance of teaching proportional reasoning to our pupils, but they do demonstrate that whilst inside the classroom problems are often selected in the service of the mathematics, outside mathematics is more frequently utilised in the service of a problem.

Teaching mathematics in a cross-curricular way, then, can help to familiarise pupils with the idea of applying mathematics in context, encouraging them to develop the skills of selecting appropriate mathematics, applying it and critically evaluating its use against real concerns and limitations. The context serves to steer the mathematics, rather than just illustrate a mathematical idea. The Dutch mathematics educator Freudenthal wrote that: 'Viewing context as noise, apt to disturb the clear mathematical message, is wrong; the context itself is the message and mathematics a means of decoding' (Freudenthal 1991: 75). The ideal of preparing learners for the world by teaching them a contextualised, applied form of mathematics has clear links to many current initiatives, such as functional mathematics and work-related learning, which are examined below. The relationship between content and context, and the goal of developing skills that can transfer between situations and disciplines are both discussed further in Chapter 3.

It can also be argued that cross-curricular teaching offers the teacher opportunities to make the mathematics itself more authentic. If particular mathematical concepts were originally developed out of a recognition that a type of problem could be solved in a certain way, is it then disadvantageous, and possibly even disingenuous to remove the topic from its original purpose and not recognise its origin? Mason and Johnston-Wilder argue that:

> seeing topics arise from classes of problems suggests that the motivation for a topic can often be found in versions of the original problems that the topic resolves, and in the range of problems to which that topic can be applied in different contexts.
>
> (Mason and Johnston-Wilder 2006: 16)

Cross-curricular practice can help to embody this ideal.

Motivation

This idea leads onto a second argument that can be used to support a cross-curricular approach: that it is motivating for pupils to see how mathematics is used in other subjects and disciplines. The psychologist Bruner suggested that: 'The best way to create interest in a subject is to render it worth knowing – which means to make the knowledge gained usable in one's thinking beyond the situation in which the learning has occurred' (Bruner 1960: 31). Pupil motivation is a complex construct that is influenced by a wide range of factors and develops over time. However, educational research offers us some general principles which are relevant to cross-curricular teaching. Middleton and Spanias reviewed the research concerning motivation for achievement in mathematics and reached the following conclusion:

Providing opportunities for students to develop intrinsic motivation in mathematics is generally superior to providing extrinsic incentives for achievement. To facilitate the development of students' intrinsic motivation, teachers must teach knowledge and skills that are worth learning. In other words, students must understand that the mathematics instruction they receive is useful.

(Middleton and Spanias 1999: 81)

This is an important finding; it tells us that whilst extrinsic motivators such as grades, marks and prizes can encourage pupils in the mathematics classroom, pupils are more likely to be motivated if they can see the use in what they are doing. This idea is repeated further on: 'Last, and most important, achievement motivation in mathematics, though stable, can be affected through careful instructional design … Creating interesting contexts within which problems are situated stimulates students' imaginations and illustrates to them that mathematics is useful in various applications' (p. 82).

Teaching with an awareness of the wider curriculum allows the mathematics teacher to demonstrate the importance and relevance of mathematics, and to reveal the chameleon discipline at work. An instance of this is given in the report *Mathematics: Understanding the Score*, where a teacher is praised for the way in which they answered the question, 'Why do we have to learn algebra?'

The teacher reminded the pupils that algebra is important in science because formulae are needed to express the laws of science; spreadsheets use algebraic formulae and are a very powerful tool used by thousands of businesses; and computer graphics require complicated algebraic methods to make sure that objects are portrayed correctly. He also pointed out the power of algebraic notation as a means of communicating within mathematics.

(Ofsted 2009: 17)

Carefully constructed problem situations might even motivate the learner further, by giving them room to devise their own strategies, carry out their own methods and develop a genuine sense of ownership regarding their work. A compartmentalisation of the curriculum can work against this, as a pupil might feel limited to only using strategies and skills that they think are typical of a mathematics lesson.

Developing integrated skills

A third argument for the use of cross-curricular activity in schools is that it supports the development of skills that transcend traditional curriculum areas. These include practical skills, such as the appropriate use of technology to aid investigation, and reflective, metacognitive skills such as the ability to synthesise different techniques to develop a problem-solving strategy, and the capacity to think creatively.

An example of this type of skills-based thinking can be found in the PLTS (Personal, Learning and Thinking Skills) contained in the 2008 National Curriculum (QCA 2007). These are six groups of skills which teachers are statutorily required to integrate throughout the curriculum to support learners' development. The six groups are:

- Independent enquirers
- Creative thinkers
- Reflective learners
- Team workers
- Self-managers
- Effective participants

Whilst these skills should be encouraged in all mathematics lessons, cross-curricular activity can offer more obvious opportunities for this sort of personal development. For example, you might challenge pupils to work in groups to devise and a carry out an investigation into the relative effectiveness of three brands of kitchen roll. Alternatively, you could ask each group to research the traffic flow around the school, design one improvement to be made to the road system and then justify their choice to the rest of the class. This type of task can present explicit ways in which personal skills can be developed, and possibly even assessed.

It is important to recognise that these skills are not superficial extras, but important cognitive skills which will ultimately impact upon pupils' performance in all subjects. In the case of mathematics, these skills all contribute to a pupil's ability to solve problems and carry out mathematical investigation; there are definite links between these six groups and the 'key processes' and 'key concepts' sections of the National Curriculum programme of study for mathematics (QCA 2007: 140–144).

Reflective task

Think back to your experiences as a learner of mathematics. Did you take part in any activities or tasks that were presented to you as 'cross-curricular'? If so, did they have any impact on your learning and/or motivation to study mathematics? Were there any elements of the tasks that you think involved the PLTS given above?

The three short arguments presented above are only the beginning of the reasoning behind cross-curricular approaches to teaching and learning, but hopefully at this stage you can already see some of the value that cross-curricular methods can bring to mathematics. The National Centre for Excellence in Teaching Mathematics, in their report *Mathematics Matters* went as far as stating that 'teaching is *more effective* when it creates connections between topics both within and beyond mathematics and with the real world' (NCETM 2008: 19, emphasis added).

This view is supported by educational research. The Centre for the Use of Research and Evidence in Education summarised a number of recent studies about cross-curricular practice and made two key points that referred to mathematics teaching (Bell *et al*. 2008). First, they noted that there was lots of evidence for 'the effectiveness of learning that is "context based" (dealing with situations and phenomena in real or simulated practical situations) most notably in studies of science and maths.' Second, they found that there was a 'need to create opportunities to identify and build on pupils' existing conceptual understandings – again, notably in science and maths. Several reviewers also found evidence of unexplored poor understanding or misunderstandings arising from "teaching to the test"' (p. 3). Cross-curricular learning, then, can strengthen teaching and improve learning.

Of course, there are potential dangers too – cross-curricular projects must be pitched carefully at the right level of ability so as not to demotivate pupils, and they must also be presented as a valuable learning experience, not just a 'fun extra'. Cross-curricular activities can also be time and resource intensive, and you must strike a balance between integrating smaller cross-curricular elements into daily practice and investing in more extensive initiatives. Pupils may also need additional support if they are unused to working in a cross-curricular fashion. Some of these practical issues are addressed in more detail in Chapters 9 and 10.

Nevertheless, the discussion above makes it clear that cross-curricular teaching offers many benefits, and may even be a hallmark of more effective mathematics teaching. This argument is especially relevant at present, as there have been a number of recent developments in mathematics education which invoke cross-curricular ideas and principles. One of the most significant of these has been the revision of the English National Curriculum.

The 2008 National Curriculum

The latest edition of the English National Curriculum (QCA 2007) began to apply to schools in 2008. It contains a number of extensive changes to previous editions, most obviously the fact that the secondary curriculum is now presented as a single, tightly integrated entity: each programme of study follows a common format; every subject's curriculum is contained within a single document; even the new logo, which consists of the individual subjects' colours twisting together into a shell-like shape, reflects the increased emphasis on an integrated curriculum.

Cross-curricular teaching and learning is also explicitly mentioned in individual subjects' programmes of study. For instance, the 'curriculum opportunities' section in the mathematics programme of study includes the instruction that teachers should provide opportunities for pupils to 'work on problems that arise in other subjects and in contexts beyond the school' (Item 4d, p. 147 and p. 163). This is a statutory requirement, which means it is actually a legal obligation for schools to provide some form of cross-curricular provision. This demand has influenced the content of some newer textbook series, and is embodied in resources such as the Bowland Maths case studies, which are discussed elsewhere in this book.

The National Curriculum also includes a number of themed sets of skills and areas of study which stretch across the curriculum. As well as the PLTS described above, the National Curriculum identifies three sets of 'functional skills'. These are defined as the 'core elements of English, mathematics and ICT that provide individuals with the skills and abilities they need to operate confidently, effectively and independently in life, their communities and work' (QCA 2007, 'Functional Skills' section). Schools are required to embed these skills in all subjects across the curriculum to promote the development of competencies in literacy, numeracy and the use of ICT. These skills often work in parallel with cross-curricular goals; support and intervention resources such as *Study Plus* (DfES 2007) often contain both functional and cross-curricular elements, and extended cross-curricular activities are likely to naturally involve a range of functional skills.

Another feature of the National Curriculum that stretches across subjects is the cross-curriculum dimensions. Unlike the PLTS and functional skills, these are non-statutory - that is, they are optional enhancements to the curriculum. The reasoning behind this may involve the fact that different schools will engage with the dimensions in very different ways. The seven dimensions are presented as 'important unifying areas of learning that help young people make sense of the world and give education relevance and authenticity. They reflect the major ideas and challenges that face individuals and society' (QCA 2007, 'Cross-Curriculum Dimensions' section).

The seven cross-curriculum dimensions are:

- Identity and cultural diversity
- Healthy lifestyles
- Community participation
- Enterprise
- Global dimension and sustainable development
- Technology and media
- Creativity and critical thinking

Mathematics can play a role in the study of each of these dimensions. For example, a mathematics teacher might engage with the 'identity and cultural diversity' dimension by using summary statistics and graphical representations of data to explore the demographics of Britain, looking at age profiles, languages spoken or professed religious beliefs. They might go on to examine regional variations, or how these things have changed over time. This could then lead to a discussion about identity and diversity in modern Britain.

Practical task

Consider each of the cross-curriculum dimensions above. For each dimension, try to think of a mathematical activity that could contribute to the presentation of that dimension, and hence connect it to the mathematics programmes of study.

Finally, it is worth noting there has been a shift in the current documentation and government guidelines which allows for a greater degree of flexibility and personalisation in the way that schools present the secondary curriculum. Some schools have taken advantage of this and instituted a shorter, two-year Key Stage 3, whilst others have responded by introducing 'flexible curriculum' days, or entirely rethinking their approach to the first few years of secondary education. One example of this is the Royal Society of Arts *Opening Minds* framework (RSA 2008), which encourages schools to integrate their teaching of many subjects, and to deliver instead a curriculum themed around five competencies.

CASE STUDY: *Opening Minds*

Farnham Heath End School is a school in Surrey which is currently using the *Opening Minds* framework with their Year 7 pupils. The school's intention is to give their pupils experiences that will develop the skills and abilities that they will need in order to successfully progress in their future lives. This includes instilling the pupils with skills of enquiry and independent learning that will serve them well in all subject areas as they progress through the school.

Ten per cent of the Year 7 curriculum time is allocated to short, fast-paced projects, which are delivered across a whole day to half the year group at a time. In each project the pupils are presented with a task which they have to explore using a range of competencies and skills drawn from many different subject areas. One project, 'Trash to Treasure', challenged pupils to recycle rubbish into a saleable product. The outcomes of this product included a prototype model, a spreadsheet to demonstrate the group's projected finances and a video advertisement. Another project involved the pupils looking at affluence and poverty in London, exploring the issues and expressing their opinions through media such as art and poetry. Each project is carefully designed to be strongly cross-curricular, and not based in a single subject area, so that pupils and teachers focus on the competencies involved.

Many of the projects contain strong mathematical elements. In one project each group of pupils was asked to form their own political party and create a manifesto. As part of this the pupils had to explain in detail how they were going to raise money through different taxes, and how they were going to prioritise their spending. This required the pupils to explore the range of salaries that people in Britain typically earn and how much income tax different people might have to pay; they also had to consider additional taxes such as road tax. In this way the mathematical skills of budgeting and calculating percentages were taught in parallel with an appreciation of wider citizenship issues. Tax bills were calculated in a realistic way, and pupils could see how the financial concerns of individuals were related to items of national expenditure such as transport, defence and health care.

The pupils have responded very positively to the *Opening Minds* sessions, and seem to be developing positive learning behaviours. One pupil said that 'I enjoy working on *Opening Minds* because it is fun and sometimes hard.' Another pupil who had been identified as more able reflected that 'It is a way of having fun as well as learning. It teaches us independence and organisation skills because we are left to our own devices.' Teachers have also noticed that the scheme has had a positive effect on the pupils, observing that learners are more likely to integrate ICT into their work or evaluate their drama without being prompted. Parents of pupils at the school have also noted that the scheme has worked well and that their children are developing in confidence.

At the time of writing, the staff of Farnham Heath End are seeking to capitalise on the initial success of this initiative, and they aim to extend the scheme in some form into Year 8. At the same time, they are also seeking to strengthen the pedagogy involved. For instance, whilst self- and peer-assessment is used extensively, the staff have found that it can be challenging to assess mastery of learning competencies in a standardised way. Some pupils are also less willing to contribute than others, and there are still questions about the best way to differentiate and distribute resources. However, the staff and pupils agree that the overall experience has been an extremely valuable one that has had a positive effect on pupils' learning, engagement and self-esteem.

The content and presentation of the revised National Curriculum repeatedly demonstrates a deliberate move towards a more integrated presentation of the curriculum in schools which resonates with the definition of 'cross-curricular' discussed at the start of this chapter. In practice, this means that cross-curricular elements should become more obvious and prevalent in schemes of work in mathematics.

Alongside the changes to the National Curriculum, a number of new qualifications have been introduced recently which support cross-curricular approaches to teaching mathematics. It is worth being aware of such qualifications, as they might serve to enable and structure cross-curricular opportunities in your own practice.

Functional skills qualifications

The functional skills qualifications are intended to connect with the functional skills content of the National Curriculum. Functional mathematics can be assessed at either level 1 (comparable to a grade of D to G at GCSE) or level 2 (comparable to a grade of A★ to C at GCSE). Whilst the functional mathematics qualification exists as an additional, optional award, it also forms part of many 14–19 diploma awards (see below) and has been taken up by some adult education centres as well as schools.

The intention of these qualifications is to assess a candidate's competency with commonly used elements of mathematical content and mathematical techniques. To this end, questions on the examination papers are presented in contexts which are seen as largely practical, based in reality, and easily recognisable. Contexts used on past papers and specimen papers include completing a multi-step expenses claim form, interpreting figures and data concerning the production and consumption of coffee, and a longer task based around planning and booking a holiday abroad.

This sort of contextualised question obviously has links to a cross-curricular approach, and the intention of encouraging pupils to use mathematics appropriately in a variety of contexts is undoubtedly positive. However, whilst this style of question locates the mathematics in the real world, there is little or no synthesis of the mathematics with concepts or techniques from other subject areas. As such these qualifications, whilst positive in many respects, stop short of the full cross-curricular ideal.

14–19 diplomas

The 14–19 diplomas are another recently introduced set of qualifications which have the potential to promote cross-curricular teaching. Each diploma combines school-based study with work-based learning, with the intention of contextualising the content and motivating learners. As such they usually involve partnerships between schools, colleges and workplaces. There are 14 diploma subjects available at present, including construction and the built environment, hospitality, and sport and active leisure. Each subject can be studied at three levels: foundation (equivalent to 5 GCSEs at grades D to G,) higher (equivalent to 7 GCSEs at grades A★ to C) and advanced (equivalent to 3.5 A-levels.)

Mathematics features in these diplomas in two key ways. Most obviously, the diplomas incorporate the functional skills qualifications described above. Pupils must pass a level 1 exam in functional mathematics before they can be awarded a foundation diploma, and a level 2 exam in functional mathematics in order to obtain a higher or advanced diploma. This prerequisite reinforces the idea that the functional mathematics qualification develops a practical numeracy.

In addition, there is also a great deal of scope for incorporating mathematics into the subject-specific learning that is delivered as part of the diploma. Each of the diplomas contains some areas of study which would be enhanced and made more authentic through the use of mathematical and statistical methods. Whilst this is especially true for diplomas traditionally delivered with a quantitative accent, such as business, administration and finance, or engineering, there is scope for supporting all of these qualifications with mathematics. In fact, the potential in some cases is quite staggering; since diplomas involve real workplaces and providers from different backgrounds, there is the potential for a very high level of authenticity, and for mathematics to be presented as a worthwhile and important subject. However, it should be noted that these opportunities may not be immediately obvious to those delivering the diplomas, and unless mathematicians are involved in structuring the teaching, opportunities may be lost and the mathematics may be limited to the functional skills content.

'Use of mathematics' and 'use of statistics' A-levels

Perhaps the most substantial recent additions to the range of qualifications available in mathematics are the new A-level qualifications in the 'use of mathematics' and the 'use of statistics'. These have also been the most controversial.

The introduction of 'use of mathematics' qualifications arose out of the dual concerns that not enough pupils were studying mathematics post-16, and that many other subjects included a significant mathematical component that was proving problematic for pupils not taking A-level mathematics. The 'use of…' qualifications were originally conceived of as Level 3 FSMQs, or free-standing mathematics qualifications, which meant that a pupil could study a single module such as 'using and applying statistics', or 'modelling with calculus' and receive accreditation for it. As further motivation, certain combinations of three modules could be combined to create an AS-level qualification. The intention was that the smaller modules would be of more interest, and seem more manageable to pupils who wanted to study some mathematics post-16 but did not want to commit to a full A-level. In some cases these FSMQs might offer support to higher level qualifications such as the advanced diplomas.

These modules were conceived of, and generally delivered, in a strongly cross-curricular way. Each skill was motivated by its practical use in real-life fields and the supporting materials illustrated the curriculum with a wide variety of substantial contexts. The commitment to developing learners who have a cross-curricular understanding of mathematics was most strongly underlined by the inclusion of a coursework portfolio which accounted for half of the final grade. This was made up of pieces of the pupil's work which demonstrated their ability to apply mathematics in real-life situations, often of the pupil's own choosing. (The assessment regulations have now changed due to wider concerns, and most modules are now assessed solely with a written terminal examination.)

The new qualification structure intended for September 2011 includes a much wider range of modules, including new modules built around finance and modules that are rated as A2-level, rather than AS-level. This arrangement allows for pupils to combine certain combinations of six units into a full A-level in either 'use of mathematics' or 'use of statistics'. It is this possibility which has caused heated debate in the mathematics education community.

The applied nature of these modules means that there is a greater emphasis on the development of skills in the application of mathematics, and the ability to critically evaluate the use of mathematics in modelling a real-life problem. However, in order to make room for the practice and development of these skills, the 'use of...' modules have a reduced content in comparison to A-level mathematics modules. Some groups (for example MEI 2009) have expressed a concern that as a result centres might begin to offer A-level use of mathematics instead of A-level mathematics, and that there would be a consequent reduction in the mathematical competence of many undergraduates.

The desire to provide mathematics qualifications that appeal to a large number of people is often in tension with concerns about 'dumbing down' and maintaining standards. Awarding bodies have to balance the amount of content they expect pupils to know with the level of mastery they expect them to demonstrate. You will have to consider similar issues in your own cross-curricular practice, so it will be interesting to see how the 'use of...' qualifications develop over the coming years.

Practical task

Every mathematics department will have a different view on the value of cross-curricular teaching and learning in mathematics, and how such teaching should be integrated into practice. If you are currently teaching at a school, you may find it useful to do a brief cross-curricular audit before reading any further.

- Are cross-curricular opportunities referenced in the departmental schemes of work? Try to look at sample schemes from Key Stages 3, 4 and 5 and compare them.

- What resources are available for cross-curricular work? Do these tend to support shorter, integrated cross-curricular contexts, or longer, more involved cross-curricular projects and initiatives?

- Finally, which (if any) of the qualifications discussed above does your department offer? Are they offered to all learners, or just some? You might like to talk to your Head of Department about their experience of these qualifications, and the impact they have on learners.

Cross-curricular mathematics in primary schools

No survey of the cross-curricular landscape would be complete without some mention of current practice in primary schools. Although primary schools are often seen as places where cross-curricular projects and topic work are much more prevalent, this is not always the case, particularly where mathematics is concerned. Since the introduction of the numeracy hour, many primary schools have moved away from integrating substantial mathematical aspects into their topic work, and have separated mathematics off in order to make sure that they are meeting the statutory requirements.

This is not true of all primary schools, of course, and many continue to incorporate mathematical thinking and ideas into their projects. In addition, cross-curricular mathematics in primary schools is strongly emphasised in the 'mathematical understanding' section of the new National Curriculum primary handbook (QCDA 2010). This contains a discrete, explicit section on 'cross-curricular studies':

This area of learning should provide opportunities for:
a) children to develop and apply their literacy, numeracy and ICT skills
b) personal, emotional and social development
c) enhancing children's mathematical understanding through making links to other areas of learning and to wider issues of interest and importance.

(QCDA 2010: 45)

What is important to recognise as a secondary mathematics teacher is that pupils will arrive in the secondary school with varied experiences of cross-curricular work. Some will arrive with an existing appreciation of the role of mathematics in supporting and working alongside other subjects, whereas others will find many of the ideas and approaches you are promoting unfamiliar. This may have implications for your choice of approach.

Finding your own context for cross-curricular mathematics

This chapter began by considering what it meant for teaching and learning to be 'cross-curricular', and went on to examine some of the ways in which cross-curricular practice can enter the contemporary mathematics classroom. In many ways there has never been a more exciting time to be a mathematics teacher with cross-curricular aspirations; the resources, technology and qualifications available are both wide-ranging and inspiring.

However, if you are just starting out as a teacher the sheer scope and number of these opportunities can seem daunting – should you attempt to start a three-week project in collaboration with the music department, or try and introduce a functional skills programme into your school? Is it enough to introduce occasional contexts that are drawn from other subjects into your lessons, or do you need to deliver a markedly different curriculum?

At this stage you are encouraged only to consider those ideas and practices that you feel fit with your developing identity as a practitioner. As you read through this book you will find some ideas more appealing than others, either for reasons of merit, or because you feel they fit more comfortably with your own personal teaching style. Still, it is important to keep in mind the principles of cross-curricular teaching and learning laid out in this introductory chapter:

- Does the activity involve a genuine transfer and synthesis of knowledge, skills and understanding?
- Does it enrich pedagogy?
- Finally, does it result in an enhanced experience for the learner?

Repeatedly asking these questions of your own teaching as you read through this book will help you develop your own perspective on authentic cross-curricular teaching and learning in mathematics.

The next chapter in this book will help you further in this respect by posing the question, 'What makes mathematics special?' Mathematics is awarded a particular value by both the current English educational system and wider society, and considering why that might be the case will offer some insight into what mathematics can offer to other curricular areas.

After this, each of the next six chapters examines a specific issue that affects cross-curricular approaches, and illustrates this issue with examples, case studies and ideas clustered around a particular subject or group of subjects. Chapter 3 begins by looking at the question of skill and knowledge transfer with a focus on the sciences – why is it that some pupils can perform a task or procedure in one subject and then fail to do so in another? How do we make sense of a pupil who can draw a graph in mathematics, but not in biology? Chapter 4 looks at the technology subjects and considers how pupils' access to physical and virtual constructions can develop their understanding of mathematical concepts.

Chapter 5 looks at how mathematics can help develop pupils as critical citizens, and how social and ethical questions can enter into mathematics lessons, forming links with subjects such as English, citizenship and geography. It also considers the roles of writing and talk in the mathematics classroom. Chapter 6 goes on to examine how multiple cultures have contributed to the development of mathematics, and how a cross-cultural and historical understanding of mathematics as a human discipline can draw on subjects such as history, RE and art.

Chapter 7 then looks at the issues of 'symbol sense' and mathematical modelling, and discusses how algebra is used in a wide number of disciplines. This leads to connections with ICT, business studies and economics. Next, Chapter 8 looks at how pedagogic approaches can also cross curricular boundaries, and asks whether we might improve our mathematics teaching by incorporating strategies from the performing arts subjects of drama, dance and music. Chapter 9 looks at the modern foreign language subjects and PE, examining some of the practical concerns and pitfalls surrounding cross-curricular provision, before Chapter 10 asks 'What comes next?'

To aid your ongoing professional development, each chapter in this book, and the accompanying titles within the series, ends with an outline of how the text and activities contained within it contribute toward the Q standards. This is intended as a guideline for you to link your work to your wider development.

Professional Standards for QTS

This chapter will help you meet the following Q standards: Q6, Q7, Q8, Q10, Q11, Q14, Q15.

Professional Standards for Teachers

This chapter will help you meet the following core standards: C6, C7, C8, C11, C14, C15, C16.

Further reading

QCA (2007) *The National Curriculum: Statutory Requirements for Key Stages 3 and 4.*
The online support for the National Curriculum is extensive and encourages teachers to forge cross-curricular links in a number of ways. The resources provided include case studies of cross-curricular mathematics lessons and a subject comparison tool which allows teachers to directly compare elements of different subjects' programmes of study. It is worthwhile spending some time looking at the online support provided for initiatives such as functional skills, PLTS and the cross-curriculum dimensions to familiarise yourself with their role in the mathematics curriculum and how they might be used as a starting point for cross-curricular provision.
Savage, J. (2011) *Cross-Curricular Teaching and Learning in the Secondary School.*
The generic book in this series goes into more detail about the role that cross-curricular teaching can play in motivating learners and enhancing their school experience.

2

Where does mathematics belong? Placing mathematics in a twenty-first century curriculum

It is easy to argue that mathematics plays a major role in our modern society; in fact, it is hard to avoid reaching this conclusion. As an example, consider the journey that a teacher has to undertake. To be admitted onto a teacher training course, you have to demonstrate a certain level of mathematical ability. In order to qualify, you have to pass a numeracy skills test. You then end up working in schools which are judged on their GCSE results – with particular weighting given to the subjects of English and … mathematics. This experience is common to teachers of all subjects, not just mathematics specialists. Whilst it might be a cliché, it is certainly true that 'maths counts'.

Yet at the same time there is a definite stigma attached to mathematics. Whilst people are usually ashamed to admit they are illiterate, they are more likely to admit that they 'don't get on with numbers'. The relationships that pupils develop with mathematics at school are often complex and contradictory, and these can carry on into adult life.

This chapter will look at some of the reasons that our society attaches such importance to mathematics, and explore how an appreciation of these reasons can inform the way that you identify opportunities for cross-curricular teaching and learning. It will also question whether authentic cross-curricular activity might challenge, or even prevent, some of the negative beliefs that people hold about mathematics.

Key objectives

By the end of this chapter, you will have:

- Considered some of the reasons why mathematics holds a special place in the secondary curriculum, and critically evaluated their validity in the twenty-first century
- Explored how these reasons can highlight opportunities for cross-curricular approaches in mathematics
- Thought about the ways in which pupils develop negative perceptions of mathematics, and whether cross-curricular activity might help improve some learners' perceptions of the subject

Why is mathematics a 'core' subject?

Along with English and science, mathematics is considered to be a 'core' subject in the English education system; it is also one of one three subjects that are said to contain 'functional skills'. It is often awarded an extra level of attention within schools; it frequently receives extra funding from local authorities; and it usually takes up a much larger proportion of the school timetable than most other subjects. What reasons are there behind this bias? In short, why is mathematics a 'core' subject?

Reflective task (Part 1)

Before reading any further, imagine that you have been asked by a pupil why mathematics is a core subject. Briefly write down three or four reasons that you might give as part of your answer.

One argument is that mathematics has always been awarded a certain respect throughout the history of formal education in England. This is certainly true to some extent. However, the mathematics taught today is far removed from the limited content that is reported in historical accounts. For instance, arithmetic was originally introduced as an applied skill, helping priests to calculate dates for Easter, and it was not compulsory for public schools to teach arithmetic until 1862 (Howson 1982). Historical factors cannot fully account for the influence that mathematics has today.

Another argument holds that mathematics is awarded a special place in the school curriculum because it leads to qualifications that are very important for both learners and the school. In particular, a grade C or above in GCSE mathematics acts as a gatekeeper qualification for many opportunities in employment and further education, and the proportion of pupils who achieve this target is used as a statistic by which schools are publicly judged. Whilst there are many good reasons that mathematics might have initially been chosen for use as a gatekeeper subject (some of which are discussed below), it is valid to question whether this situation is self-perpetuating. Could it be that originally society attached value to a mathematics qualification because it saw the subject of mathematics as important – but now it views the learning of mathematics in school as important because of the value of the qualification? It is valuable to ask questions like this, as they can offer some insight into the confusing and contradictory opinions that your pupils might hold with regard to mathematics. In addition, it also gives rise to a number of other valuable socio-political questions about the teaching and learning of mathematics and its position in the curriculum (for example, see Noyes 2007).

The argument that informs cross-curricular practice most closely, though, is that mathematics as a discipline has a number of qualities which are extensive in their reach and critical for every learner. This is the claim presented by the English National Curriculum, which begins its programmes of study for mathematics by outlining the importance of the subject:

Mathematical thinking is important for all members of a modern society as a habit of mind for its use in the workplace, business and finance; and for personal decision-making.

Mathematics is fundamental to national prosperity in providing tools for understanding science, engineering, technology and economics. It is essential in public decision-making and for participation in the knowledge economy.

Mathematics equips pupils with uniquely powerful ways to describe, analyse and change the world. It can stimulate moments of pleasure and wonder for all pupils when they solve a problem for the first time, discover a more elegant solution, or notice hidden connections. Pupils who are functional in mathematics and financially capable are able to think independently in applied and abstract ways, and can reason, solve problems and assess risk.

Mathematics is a creative discipline. The language of mathematics is international. The subject transcends cultural boundaries and its importance is universally recognised. Mathematics has developed over time as a means of solving problems and also for its own sake.

(QCA 2007: 139)

This is a considered statement which connects the place of mathematics as a discipline with the wider aims of the current version of the National Curriculum. It is worth reading this a few times, and considering how closely it reflects your own views.

Reflective task (Part 2)

Reread the 'importance of mathematics' statement printed above. Now compare this quote with your answers from the first part of this task. Do your answers relate to ideas in all three of the paragraphs in the statement?

Which of the points in the National Curriculum statement do you think you most strongly agree with at the moment? Are there any sentences which you disagree with? Are there any points which you think are noticeably absent from the statement?

There are three important strands of argument which can be identified to varying extents in the National Curriculum statement. The first is that mathematics can function as a toolkit for use in other disciplines. The second is that mathematics is required for individuals to successfully navigate a number of everyday and common situations. The third strand argues that mathematics develops the human mind and equips it to interpret and interact with the world. These themes are neither exhaustive nor mutually exclusive, but they offer three very important rationales that all support a cross-curricular approach to the teaching and learning of mathematics.

Mathematics as a toolkit

Throughout history, many different metaphors have been used to describe the nature and purpose of mathematics. One of the most common is the idea that mathematics is a toolkit, made up of a number of techniques and methods that can be used in a large number of ways, and in an even larger number of situations. For example, trigonometry is a technique used in navigation, astronomy and engineering. The tools of calculus can be used to find the flux of electromagnetic fields, to calculate marginal costs in economics or to investigate the rate of change of an insect population. When mathematics is thought of in this way, it is natural to use contexts from outside of mathematics in the classroom in order to illustrate why a subject is being taught, and how a particular 'tool' might be applied. If these contexts are introduced in an authentic and substantial way, they will lead to cross-curricular experiences.

An example that pupils might be familiar with from technology is that whenever two resistors are connected together in parallel, their combined resistance can be calculated by using the following formula:

$$\frac{1}{R_T} = \frac{1}{R_1} + \frac{1}{R_2}$$

where R_1 and R_2 refer to the values of the individual resistors, and R_T gives the value of the combined resistance. This context illustrates the tool of adding fractions, and could be used to enhance a mathematics lesson. To make their lesson more authentically cross-curricular, the teacher might use common resistor values, such as $100\,\Omega$ or $220\,\Omega$ and, if appropriate, consider more complicated situations such as circuits where resistors are combined variously in both series and parallel. Other mathematical tools could be introduced by looking at the percentage tolerances on individual resistors and investigating the percentage error of different combinations of resistors.

A less familiar example of mathematics being used as a toolkit comes from epidemiology, the study of illness and disease. Epidemiologists describe each contagious disease with a parameter known as the basic reproduction number, or R_0. This is the average number of people that an infected person will infect before recovering or dying, assuming that no one in the population is immune. Different diseases have different values: airborne measles has a value between 12 and 18, whilst smallpox has a R_0 value between 5 and 7. The R_0 value for the recent 2009 outbreak of swine flu is still being calculated, but estimates at the time of writing place it between about 1.4 and 1.6. This is comparable to values calculated for standard seasonal influenza.

This key value allows us to model the spread of diseases using the mathematical tools of sequences and series. Using geometric progressions, pupils can model what will happen when diseases have R_0 values that are less than 1, or more than 1. The teacher can also construct specific scenarios: if a single person was infected with a disease which had an R_0 value of 2, and on average the infection spreads every six hours, how many people would you expect to be infected at the end of the week?

Again, our desire for authentic cross-curricular practice will encourage us to pose questions about the limitations of this model, and raise the issue of how it might be developed further. One additional angle would be to consider the fact that some diseases (such as sexually transmitted infections) have different R_0 values for different groups within the population, and bring in questions of health and personal behaviours. Mathematics does not always have the ability to answer such delicate questions, but if a situation can be quantified, insight can often be gained through the use of mathematical tools.

The ideal of mathematics as a toolkit is particularly relevant in the current climate. 'Applied mathematics' used to be used as a synonym for mechanics (mathematical physics), or later for mechanics and statistics. However, the rapid development of technology and its widespread use in society has generated a huge number of applications of mathematics across a number of technical fields: CCTV image enhancement, Internet cryptography, mobile phone signal triangulation, and computer-generated imagery in films and television programmes all use mathematics.

Furthermore, whilst the National Curriculum states that mathematics provides 'tools for understanding science, engineering, technology and economics,' its influence actually stretches much further, well beyond the traditional STEM (science, technology, engineering and mathematics) bracket of subjects. Operations research uses mathematical algorithms to improve efficiency in fields such as logistics and management science. Social sciences such as psychology and sociology use statistics extensively in their research. Newer areas of mathematics such as game theory and network analysis have applications in fields as diverse as philosophy, politics and biology.

Some of these applications are positively surprising, such as the use of mathematics in criminal investigations. The American television programme *Numb3rs* has done much to publicise this, and whilst the programme might occasionally stretch the truth for dramatic purposes, the programme is based on genuine techniques and uses mathematics consultants to help ensure a fair level of realism (Devlin and Lorden 2007).

A possible rule of thumb is that wherever there is:

- quantification
- measurement
- pattern spotting (and extrapolation)
- the idea of distribution and error

there is the potential for mathematical tools to be applied to describe a situation, and in many cases, to help solve related problems.

Practical task (Part 1)

Pupils often ask why they are required to learn algebra. How might you answer this question by thinking about mathematics as a toolkit? Try to think of three or four contexts that you could give as part of your answer. Could any of these be developed into a cross-curricular activity?

Presenting the toolkit

The discussion above only touches on the plethora of uses that mathematics has in the modern world. Yet despite this abundance of applications, pupils often hold a limited view of mathematics, and the role that it plays in the 'real world'.

Picker and Berry (2000) conducted some research into the images that lower secondary age pupils held about mathematicians. Their findings suggested the existence of a number of strong stereotypes about both mathematicians and mathematics. Mathematics largely came across as a narrow and limited discipline. When asked to give a reason that someone might hire a mathematician, many pupils left their papers blank. The top four answers given by pupils in the United Kingdom were: accounting, teaching, banking and programming (pp. 71–72). It would appear that many pupils are not being made aware of the size and power of the mathematical toolkit.

There are many possible reasons for this. Pupils' impressions of mathematics are undoubtedly influenced by the way that mathematics is presented on television, and also by how they see their parents and peers engaging with the subject. However, it is also possible that negative perceptions about the usefulness of mathematics are perpetuated through the way that mathematics is demonstrated in the classroom. In particular, it is possible that sometimes we suggest that mathematics is not useful by offering pupils examples that are closer to 'cons' than 'contexts' (Ward-Penny 2010).

For example, consider the model question where a pupil is told that a ladder is standing against a wall. The ladder is 7 metres long, and the ladder reaches 6.4 metres up the side of the wall. How far away from the base of the wall is the bottom of the ladder? This scenario is rather disingenuous: if you have the ability to measure 6.4 metres up the side of the wall, can you not measure the required distance directly? Furthermore, why would you need this distance?

A second common type of question is the ridiculous statistic. This question is phrased in this manner: 'There are 70 people in the theatre, and 28 of them have blonde hair. What percentage does not have blonde hair?' It is understandable that these kinds of illustration find their way into mathematics teaching, but illustration is not a substitute for context. Questions like this pay lip-service to mathematics as an applied discipline but in fact reinforce the opposite impression. Genuine cross-curricular experiences can be, of course, a most effective antidote to this situation.

False applications of mathematics can encourage pupils to focus on 'playing the game', and teach them to respond to real situations in distinctly unreal ways. This practice can be demotivating for all pupils, but it has been suggested that it has a particularly adverse effect on girls' achievement and attainment (Boaler 1994). It is important, therefore, to present the toolkit in a realistic way that integrates common sense, authentic activity and contexts that have meaning for the pupils.

'Everyday' mathematics and numeracy

The discussion above answers the question of why mathematics is considered as 'core' by demonstrating that mathematics has a wide range of applications in many other disciplines, and as such it will be something that is necessary for the development of these disciplines; in the words of the National Curriculum statement, it is 'fundamental to national prosperity'. However, the presentation of mathematics as a subject-spanning toolkit does not consider the role that mathematics has at the level of the individual.

A focus on the individual gives rise to a second, complementary reason why mathematics can be considered a 'core' subject. It can be argued that contemporary society requires each individual to have a level of basic mathematics in order to function at both work and home. This 'basic' mathematics has been labelled in a number of ways: one approach is to call it 'everyday' mathematics; another is to use the expression 'functional mathematics'; and a third is to use the term numeracy, itself a word with various interpretations. In any case, a useful parallel can be drawn by thinking of people with this level of mathematical competence as being numerically literate. Typical goals of this sort of mathematics would include:

- Having confidence to give and check change in shops
- Being able to read and understand utility bills
- Reading scales on kitchen measuring instruments
- Being able to compare mobile phone tariffs
- Understanding percentage discounts in the supermarket

Whilst these goals may seem simple when compared to some of the content of the curriculum, a large number of adults do not feel confident using mathematics in this way. In a 2008 survey carried out by learndirect (learndirect 2008), 25 per cent of the adults asked said that they found it confusing comparing different gas, electric and mobile tariffs to find the best value for money, and 13 per cent said that they found it confusing working out which of two packs in the supermarket was better value if the packs were of different weights. At work, 18 per cent admitted that they relied on someone else to do calculations either 'always or sometimes'.

Other research evidence goes further towards highlighting the value of numeracy and mathematics in the work place. A study by Parsons and Bynner (2006) suggests that not only does poor numeracy have a negative effect on employment opportunities, but also that it has more of an effect than poor literacy, particularly for women. At the other end of the scale, Dolton and Vignoles (2002) found that workers with mathematics A-level earn between 7 per cent and 10 per cent more than those with similar qualifications, even when initial ability is taken into account.

There are many possible reasons that could help to explain why pupils often leave school without the confidence and ability to apply what is often seen as relatively straightforward mathematics. One possibility is that when topics are taught in a largely abstract way that is divorced from real situations, pupils do not construct knowledge in a way that will serve them well in the future. (This issue is discussed further in the next chapter.) A second possibility is that many pupils leave school having developed a degree of mathematics anxiety.

Mathematics anxiety is a genuine psychological phenomenon which manifests as a 'feeling of tension and anxiety that interferes with the manipulation of numbers and the solving of mathematical problems in a wide variety of ordinary life and academic situations' (Richardson and Suinn 1972: 551). Interestingly, research into mathematics anxiety has found that although mathematics anxiety is moderately correlated with anxiety about tests, it is not strongly correlated with measures of intelligence such as IQ (for a summary of these results, see Ashcraft and Ridley 2005). In other words, mathematics carries with it a particular set of stresses which can affect high achievers and low achievers alike. It is unclear at this time exactly what causes mathematics anxiety, but it is known that viewing intelligence as an incremental quantity and not a fixed one can help promote a more positive attitude towards learning (Dweck 2000; Lee 2009). It is also evident that certain teaching strategies can help pupils to develop a mathematical resilience (Johnston-Wilder and Lee 2010).

The research presented above can be seen as suggesting that the current system is failing to prepare many pupils for using mathematics in their everyday lives. Cross-curricular opportunities can redress this balance, by using everyday tasks as a starting point and preparing pupils through authentic practice. Cross-curricular activities that involve numeracy can also impact on pupils' wider mathematical learning, by demonstrating the worth of mathematics and improving learners' attitude towards the subject as a whole.

Some of these activities might have links with the non-statutory economic well-being and financial capability programme in the National Curriculum for Key Stage 3 (QCA 2007: 'Economic Wellbeing and Financial Capability' section). In the first instance this might include topics such as money management and budgeting, but it could also stretch to include a discussion of social choices in the use of money, and a discussion of risk and reward in the context of personal finance. Examples of this sort are discussed in more detail in Chapter 5.

Numeracy also has links to many other subject areas. You might consider offering pupils the chance to practice their proportional reasoning skills in a food technology situation; rather than getting them to rescale a recipe for a different number of people in theory, move into the kitchens and challenge them to do it in practice – the proof could then be literally in the pudding! As well as providing a motivational and memorable example of why mathematics is useful, this kind of activity demands the discussion a number of questions that might otherwise be glossed over in the mathematics classroom: how do we understand a demand for three-quarters of an egg? If something is twice as big, will it take twice as long to cook? Questions about scaling and relationships can introduce the idea of a formula (for example, how long does it take to cook a Christmas turkey?) and in this way cross-curricular dialogue continues between the two subjects.

Practical task (Part 2)

Think again about how you might answer a pupil who asks why they have to learn algebra. What answers might you give that are based around everyday mathematics? Might any of these be developed into a cross-curricular idea that could be used in a lesson?

So far the position of mathematics as a core subject has been defended using two different lines of argument: that mathematics is a widely used toolkit essential for the work of other subjects; and that basic mathematics is widely embedded in peoples' everyday lives, and so it is needed for learners to function in the real world. However, neither of these arguments is comprehensive. Not all topics in the mathematics curriculum can be construed as widely used 'tools'; for example, it is very difficult (although not impossible) to argue that the alternate segment theorem is a useful 'tool' with a wide range of applications. Furthermore, whilst 'everyday' mathematics is clearly important, there is something to be said about the value of being able to think in a logical and abstract way. Therefore, in order to finish our argument of why mathematics is a core subject, we must consider the idea of mathematics as a 'habit of mind'.

Mathematics as a 'habit of mind'

It has long been recognised that mathematics is something more than just an 'applied' subject; unlike the natural sciences it contains elements and ideas that are not necessarily grounded in the 'real world'. It is in this sense that modern mathematicians sometimes characterise themselves as 'pure' or 'applied'. As pupils study mathematics, they benefit not only from practising applications, but also from building up mathematical ways of thinking. The study of mathematics can develop what the National Curriculum calls a 'habit of mind'.

Mathematical thinking can be used in many ways; for example, it can serve as a powerful organisational tool. People often use mathematical or logical thinking strategies unconsciously to support their decision making at work and at home. For instance, someone cooking a complicated three course meal, or overseeing a project at work has to order and manage a number of events in order to meet a deadline with limited resources, time and manpower. Formally this involves what is known as critical path analysis – however, most people use this type of reasoning informally. Being able to consider things with a mathematical 'habit of mind' can improve the quality and reliability of this informal reasoning.

This type of discussion gives rise to a challenging question: does mathematics develop pupils' thinking in a way that other subjects do not? Is there something special, or even unique about the processes involved in mathematical thinking? (Skemp 1986; Tall 1991) Whilst these questions are open to much debate, it is certain that mathematics can help develop a way of thinking which is widely applicable in other subject areas, and also in later life. Furthermore, it can be argued that in much the same way that numeracy enables people to understand and carry out basic tasks involving numbers and mathematics, mathematical thinking is a prerequisite for people to function fully as critical citizens in modern society.

The final part of this chapter will look at how some of the different branches of mathematics can contribute to this claim. In a similar manner to the National Curriculum it will consider four different areas: number, algebra, geometry and statistics.

Appreciation of number

At the time of writing, the United Kingdom is in the middle of a recession, and economic headlines are frequently in the news. One of the stories that was in the news on the day that this chapter was written stated that 'the UK inflation rate rose to 3.5% in January – the fastest annual pace for 14 months – from 2.9% the month before, official figures have shown' (BBC News 2010). To understand this story, the reader has to first be comfortable with the idea of percentages. Then, in order to understand the rate of change of inflation, they must also conceptualise the second derivative of measures such as the retail prices index and the consumer prices index. This is a significant demand.

Sometimes it is the numbers within stories themselves that can be misleading. The terms 'million' and 'billion' are interchangeable to many people's ears – even though one number is one thousand times as large as the other. Douglas Hofstadter coined the phrase 'number numbness' (Hofstadter 1986: 115–135) to describe people's apparent inability to distinguish between very large and very small numbers.

A full appreciation of number involves more than just a correct perspective of size, though; it is important that people are also able to establish what numbers *mean*. Blastland and Dilnot (2008:18–19) give the example of a promise made by the British government to spend an extra £300 million on childcare over five years, in order to create a million new places. This seems like a vast amount of money, but some simple arithmetic provides a damning critique: £300 million for a million places equates to £300 per place. Given that this money has been pledged over five years, this is an average of £60 per place, per year, which is equivalent to £1.15 per week – very cheap childcare indeed!

Examples such as these demonstrate the importance of pupils developing a sense and appreciation of number. They also give rise to a number of cases where cross-curricular topics could be used to illustrate, motivate and enhance mathematics teaching and learning. Contexts such as national debt, government investment, or even the meanings of 'milligram' and 'microgram' on the side of a mineral water bottle can all find their way into the mathematics classroom.

Algebraic reasoning

The key elements of algebraic thinking are abstraction and generalisation. Even though many people might not explicitly utilise the symbolic system of letters, numbers and brackets taught at school, they regularly use the same thought processes that these symbols invoke.

The Egyptian mathematics educator Gattegno demonstrated this point by arguing that language involves symbolic abstraction:

> Abstraction makes life easy, makes it possible … Language is conveniently vague so that the word car, for example, could cover all cars, not just one. So anyone who has learned to speak, demonstrates that he can use classes, concepts … The essential point is this: algebra is an attribute, a fundamental power, of the mind. Not of mathematics only.
>
> (Gattegno 1970: 23–24)

Abstraction, then, is endemic throughout all subjects, whether through the use of language, terminology that involves categories and classification, or even in the deployment of subject-specific symbolic notation, such as in music or dance.

Both abstraction and generalisation are also important when constructing and evaluating arguments. For example, a politician on the television news might be filmed talking about the poor quality of school buildings in England whilst standing against a background of a rundown school building. Whilst the politician's statements are likely to be general in their scope, the visual image is strictly specific. This does not negate the validity of the argument, but it could be that the politician is encouraging the viewer to falsely move from the specific to the general.

In this way an explicit appreciation of the relationship between the specific and general can be politically enabling. The teaching and learning of algebra, and algebraic proof, can develop analytical tools that are used in subjects such as persuasive writing in English, and assessing and developing argument in critical thinking.

Practical task (Part 3)

For a third, and final time, return to the pupil who has asked why they have to learn algebra. Do you think the idea of mathematics as a 'habit of mind' provides any additional reasons for the study of algebra? How might you express these in a way that a school-age pupil might appreciate?

Geometrical thinking

No summary of the types of mathematical thinking engendered in the classroom would be complete without some discussion of spatial reasoning. Although some elements of early geometry teaching can be static and definition based, classroom exploration of shape and space has the potential to be filled with investigations, dynamic imagery and 'what if' questions.

This is especially true when pupils meet the idea of loci, the pathways that objects take through time. Some loci are fairly straightforward, such as the locus of the base of a pendulum, which is an arc of a circle. However, many real-life situations require significant visualisation. This visualisation becomes much more difficult when it takes place over time, or in three dimensions.

Practical task

Try each of these problems involving shape and space. As you attempt the problems, consider your own thought processes. Do you find these kinds of questions easy or difficult? Do you think mathematics develops this type of thinking?

a) As a car passes over a stone, it becomes stuck in one of the car's tyres. If the car continues on in a straight line, draw the pathway that the stone will now follow.

b) Imagine a cube made of modelling clay, sitting on a table. If we cut the cube in half by cutting in a plane parallel to the table, the shape of the cut will be a square. What other two-dimensional shapes could you make by cutting the cube in a different way?

c) Imagine a white ball suspended in mid-air. How many red balls, all of the same size as the white ball, could you arrange around it so that each of the red balls touches the white ball?

An ability to visualise accurately in this way can have benefits in a number of other curriculum areas including dance, engineering and physics.

Statistical literacy and probabilistic understanding

Mathematical thinking also includes a capacity to critically use and interpret data, summary statistics, graphs and charts. These skills are critical in modern society; the phrase 'lies, damned lies and statistics' is sadly indicative of the way that this area of mathematics is used today. It is outside the scope of this chapter to describe the ways in which people can lie with statistics in detail, and it will have to suffice to list some of the most common:

■ Constructing suspicious samples of indeterminate size
■ Using biased, leading or confusing questions to gather data

- Selectively choosing which average (mean, median or mode) to use in a report, with no indication of which one has been used or why

- Equating correlation with causation

- Constructing graphs with incomplete labels and/or truncated axes

These are clear and present dangers, and it does not take too much effort to find examples of each of these in newspapers or in media reports. The habit of critical statistical thinking, then, is important for pupils to navigate current affairs, as well as to proceed in subjects such as geography, business studies and sociology.

Modern society also requires that pupils have some facility with probabilistic reasoning. Adults frequently have to make decisions that involve a consideration of risk and reward, and an understanding of probability can provide a framework with which to explore these situations in a rational way. Possessing knowledge of probability does not necessarily force people to make a particular action – many mathematicians still play the lottery, despite knowing the odds – but it does allow people to make a more informed decision.

Probability can sometimes provide an additional way to question statistics. Dewdney (1993: 50) offers the following example, taken from a Swedish newspaper:

Last year 35 people drowned in boating accidents. Only five were wearing life jackets. The rest were not. Always wear life jackets when boating.

This is sensible advice, but mathematically it is misleading. The implication is that six times as many people drowned without a life jacket, so wearing a life jacket is six times as safe. However, this may not be the case, as we do not know what proportion of Swedes wear life jackets whilst boating. Imagine that only five boating Swedes had worn life jackets during the year in question, and that hundreds chose not to; suddenly wearing a life jacket seems like a dangerous choice! This of course was not the case, but it illustrates how statistics and probability could have been used to mislead. This sort of conditional probability is key in situations such as the medical testing of new drugs and treatments.

A more shocking example can be drawn from the case of Sally Clark, a British woman who was accused of murdering her two children in 1998. Both children had died from sudden infant death syndrome (SIDS). Since it is so rare for a cause of death to be attributed to SIDS for one child, the prosecution proposed that the probability of two such deaths was 1 in 73 million. However, there is strong reason to suppose that the deaths would not be statistically independent – that if one child had died in this way, the second would be at a greater risk – and so the theoretical probability would be substantially lower.

If we do not encourage pupils to develop a critical eye for misleading reports and probabilities we allow them to be hoodwinked, often on high stakes issues. Contemporary debates on topics such as global warming and the supposed link between autism and the MMR vaccine openly use techniques and concepts from statistics and probability, so it is important that pupils have the mathematical facility to engage with these ideas. In terms of cross-curricular potential, this 'habit of mind' has connections to many subjects, including media studies, history and topics in diplomas such as public services.

The discussions above have illustrated how mathematical thinking is an extremely powerful habit of mind. Although the individual techniques and 'tools' considered earlier have a wide range of applications, it is also incredibly valuable for a learner to possess an ability to look at situations through the lens of mathematics, whether this involves finding the meaning of some key numbers, switching between the general and the specific in an argument, visualising a object moving in three dimensions or critically examining the statistics used in the presentation of a case.

Wherever there is:

■ decision making being made within constraints

■ the use of numbers or statistics to summarise or convince

■ an appeal to evidence and the idea of the general and the specific

■ logical argument or 'proof'

■ a need for visualisation of shapes and physical behaviours

mathematical thinking skills are being called upon and exercised in some sense; bringing these out explicitly can sometimes benefit both mathematics and the subject area that these skills have been embedded in.

Mathematics as a 'core' subject

This chapter began by questioning why mathematics is awarded special status as a 'core' subject in the English National Curriculum. Thinking of mathematics as a toolkit, as a facilitator of numeracy and as a habit of mind can help to structure a substantive answer to this question. These three perspectives also offer three distinct ways in which cross-curricular opportunities in mathematics can be identified, and it is worth sharing these understandings with teachers of other subjects to see if they can identify how mathematics and mathematical thinking are relevant to them.

Before concluding, however, it is important to recognise the need to hold these three ideas of mathematics in balance. Each contains implicit ideas about what mathematics is, and how it should be understood, and overemphasising one at the expense of the others could lead to problems in the classroom.

For example, the idea of mathematics as a toolkit is widely promoted by some groups in industry, and when pupils are interested in the contexts being discussed it can enhance motivation in the classroom. However, presenting mathematics as nothing more than a set of techniques can give rise to rote-learning and depersonalisation, characteristics that in turn lead to disaffection (Nardi and Steward 2003). Presenting mathematics as a habit of mind that serves as a problem-solving tool can add balance to this type of situation. Equally, focusing on everyday mathematical concepts can be fruitful, but there is also a place for presenting highly abstract ideas and portraying mathematics as a discipline which is worthy of study in and of itself. Striking this balance is a significant challenge, one which is particularly relevant for the teacher who is seeking to integrate cross-curricular opportunities.

It is also critical to recognise the importance and validity of other disciplines. Although mathematics is a core subject, it is not the only subject; even though mathematics offers an insightful 'habit of mind', it is not always appropriate to use it. There is a certain intellectual value attached to the quantifiable which can overshadow insights offered by other disciplines; it is often assumed that 'right brained' is automatically 'right thinking'.

This is not the case, and cross-curricular activity often needs to recognise, integrate and, in some instances, defer to creative, intuitive and emotional thinking, particularly in situations where mathematics is being used in a situation with spiritual, moral, ethical or social components. This issue is discussed in more detail in Chapter 5.

The definition of cross-curricular activity at the start of Chapter 1 held that cross-curricular approach 'is characterised by sensitivity towards, and a synthesis of, knowledge, skills and understandings from various subject areas'. The knowledge, skills and understandings contained within mathematics are both remarkable and wide-ranging, and it is this fact which makes mathematics both 'core' and highly suitable for cross-curricular practice. The chapters that follow will now expand upon and exemplify this attitude, looking at the relationship that mathematics has with specific subject areas.

Professional Standards for QTS

This chapter will help you meet the following Q standards: Q14, Q15, Q23.

Professional Standards for Teachers

This chapter will help you meet the following core standards: C15, C16, C27.

Further reading

Blastland, M. and Dilnot, A. (2008) *The Tiger That Isn't*.
This popular book looks critically at recent news stories and ideas to illustrate how mathematics is sometimes used to mislead and misinform. It is packed with examples and illustrates the importance of mathematics as a critical 'habit of mind'.

Graham, A. (2006) *Developing Thinking in Statistics*.

Johnston-Wilder, S. and Mason, J. (2005) *Developing Thinking in Geometry*.

Mason, J., Graham, A. and Johnston-Wilder, S. (2005) *Developing Thinking in Algebra*.
This series of books unpacks what it means to develop 'habits of mind' in these curriculum areas; each goes beyond the content of the curriculum to provide ways in which to challenge learners' thinking.

Application and transfer: mathematics and the science subjects

Mathematics has always been closely associated with science. Skills learnt in mathematics enable progress and exploration in science, and scientific applications offer exciting examples of mathematics in action which can motivate and inspire learners of all ages. This mutually supporting relationship led the mathematician and writer E.T. Bell to describe mathematics as the 'queen and servant of science' (Bell 1951).

Yet this interdependence is not always expressed in the classroom, and students sometimes develop a compartmentalised view of the two subjects. Moreover, pupils often learn techniques such as graph drawing in mathematics then fail to use these skills appropriately in their science lessons. This phenomenon raises a critical question about both the theory and the potential of cross-curricular teaching and learning: how easy it is for pupils to transfer skills learnt in one subject to another?

This chapter outlines three theories of learning and examines the different ways in which they might begin to answer this question. It then shows how these theories offer different suggestions about how best to integrate cross-curricular links into mathematics and science lessons.

Key objectives

By the end of this chapter, you will have:

- Explored some of the links between the secondary mathematics curriculum and the curricula of physics, chemistry and biology

- Considered a number of practical barriers that could hinder cross-curricular approaches to mathematics and science

- Been introduced to the psychological idea of 'transfer' and understood how it is central to cross-curricular practice

- Read about three theories of learning: behaviourism, constructivism and situated cognition, and considered how these interpret the issue of transfer

■ Thought about a number of suggested cross-curricular activities linking mathematics and science, and started to devise some of your own

The relationship between science and mathematics

The relationship between mathematics and science is an intricate one which makes cross-curricular elements not only possible, but in some cases inevitable. In one direction, mathematics is central to much scientific activity, leading the philosopher Roger Bacon to describe mathematics in the thirteenth century AD as 'the door and key to the sciences'. More recently, the Hungarian physicist and mathematician Eugene Wigner has remarked on the 'unreasonable effectiveness of mathematics in the natural sciences' (Wigner 1960). In many fields of science, especially physics, it is impossible to demarcate where the mathematics stops and the science begins; this is also true of the mechanics modules in A-level mathematics. Joint mathematics and physics degrees are frequently offered by universities, and some teacher training centres offer a joint PGCE in mathematics and physics. On occasion, mathematics may even steer research in a scientific field, particularly within physics, with mathematical possibilities and frameworks being established first and experimental evidence and empirical proof following later.

In turn, science can justify and promote the study of mathematics. Wellington and Ireson put forward that science teaching can also improve mathematical learning: 'It could also be argued that science teachers can have a greater impact on numeracy than many other subjects. Indeed, we suggest that pupils' numeracy and wider mathematical skills can be enhanced through the study and application of science' (Wellington and Ireson 2008: 246).

The overlap between mathematics and science involves content, contexts and processes. This means that there are two main ways to connect mathematics with science in a cross-curricular manner. The first is to illustrate and give reasons for mathematical concepts by demonstrating their use in a context drawn from science. The second is to focus on skills that are used in mathematics and science, and to draw upon both subjects in order to inform pedagogy and enhance the pupils' learning experience. Although these approaches can be used profitably in unison, the next part of this chapter will consider them separately, as each involves a different set of practical and theoretical issues.

Scientific contexts for mathematics

There are literally hundreds of possible contexts that could be drawn from science to illustrate the mathematics curriculum. Three examples from each of the three science subject areas are given below; some of these are covered by the science National Curriculum, whilst others refer to ideas and topics that may not be studied until later on. You might like to consider the merits of each context, and think about which groups of pupils it might motivate.

From biology:

■ The capture-recapture (or mark and recapture) method of estimating a population size offers an interesting use of proportional reasoning. The method is illustrated most easily with an example: on a visit to an island, a biologist captures 20 turtles and marks their shells with pink paint before releasing them. On a second visit, he captures another set of 20 turtles, of which only 5 have pink paint on their shells. From this he estimates that there are 80 turtles on the island. To facilitate genuine cross-curricular thought, learners could critique the strengths and weaknesses of this technique as a method for dealing with a real-life problem. Some learners could go on to research the more mathematically refined methods which biologists have developed.

- Population dynamics can serve as an interesting context for a range of mathematical techniques. You might model the growth (or decline) of a population using sequences, compound percentage increases, or try to fit a curve to observed data. At A-level, students might like to explore the properties of the logistic differential equation:

$$\frac{dP}{dt} = rP\left(1 - \frac{P}{K}\right)$$

where P is the population size, r indicates the growth rate and K is a quantity known as the 'carrying capacity', which reflects the limits of the natural resources available. Ecological issues that can be explored using these techniques include species conservation and pest control.

- Mendel's laws of genetics offer pupils a chance to apply the ideas of probability and ratio. For the purposes of a simple example, imagine a plant with flowers that can have either blue or yellow petals. The blue trait (P) is dominant, and the yellow trait (p) is recessive. Each plant contains two alleles of the petal colour gene in its genome, and only one of these is passed on to its offspring during reproduction. Therefore, if two 'Pp' plants cross-breed, there are four possible combinations: PP, Pp, pP and pp. Since P is dominant, this leads to a 3:1 ratio of blue to yellow flowers. This cross breeding is represented using a diagram known as a Punnett square, which is structurally similar to a mathematical sample space (see Figure 3.1).

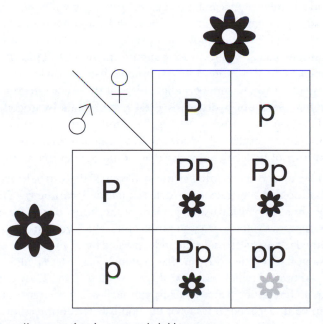

Figure 3.1 A Punnett square showing a monohybrid cross.

Follow up questions could include an exploration of what happens if you have two independent traits, what would happen in future generations, whether you would expect this ratio to be exact or approximate, and which human traits are controlled by genes with dominant and recessive alleles.

From chemistry:

- Although there are important differences in the way the word 'equation' is being used, the introduction of chemical equations into the mathematics classroom offers pupils a chance to practice their numerical reasoning. Once again, this is best illustrated with an example. Consider the reaction that occurs when methane (the primary component of natural gas) is burnt, creating carbon dioxide:

$$CH_4 + O_2 \rightarrow CO_2 + H_2O$$

This is chemically true, but the equation does not balance. On the left hand side there are four hydrogen atoms and two oxygen atoms, but on the right there are only two hydrogen atoms and one oxygen atom. Some numerical manipulation leads to the correct, amended equation:

$$CH_4 + 2O_2 \rightarrow CO_2 + 2H_2O$$

Similar balancing exercises can be constructed using the chemical equations for photosynthesis, aerobic respiration and anaerobic respiration.

- Introducing the concepts of the mole and Avogadro's number into the mathematics classroom offers pupils a chance to practice their skills of manipulating numbers in standard form whilst simultaneously developing their understanding of the scale and nature of atoms and molecules. In chemistry the mole is defined as the number of atoms present in 12 grams of Carbon 12, and Avogadro's number is defined as the number of atoms or molecules present in one mole of a substance – this has the value of 6.022×10^{23} to four significant figures. This all means that to find the weight of a single atom of a substance we can divide its standard atomic weight (usually given on the periodic table) by the Avogadro number. For example, the atomic weight of hydrogen is 1.0079, so a single hydrogen atom weighs $1.0079 \div 6.022 \times 10^{23} = 1.67 \times 10^{-24}$ kg, or a millionth of a millionth of a millionth of a thousandth of 1.67 g! More involved calculations could include calculating the number of molecules of water that would be required to make up one gram.

- Molecular geometry offers an unusual context that can be brought into the mathematics classroom to illustrate ideas such as angle and symmetry. This involves the study of the three-dimensional arrangement of the atoms that make up a molecule. A simple example is the form of a water molecule, which consists of two hydrogen atoms each joined to an oxygen molecule and separated by an angle of 104.45°. Three-dimensional examples include CH_4 (methane) which has a tetrahedral structure, SF_6 (sulphur hexafluoride) which has an octahedral structure, and IF_7 (iodine heptafluoride) which has an interesting pentagonal bi-pyramidal structure (see Figure 3.2). The geometries can be understood in terms of the bonds between the atoms, and this context could lead onto a discussion of the place and purpose of symmetry in nature.

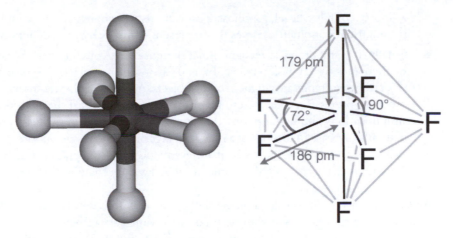

Figure 3.2 The geometric structure of iodine heptafluoride.

From physics:

■ Many contexts from physics can be used to provide real-life formulae for the teaching of algebra. A relatively complex example is the formula used to calculate the terminal velocity, V_t of a body (such as a skydiver) falling through the air, which is given by:

$$V_t = \sqrt{\frac{2mg}{\rho AC_d}}$$

where m is the mass of the object, g is the acceleration due to gravity, ρ is the density of air, A is the area of the downward face of the object and C_d is a drag coefficient. This could be used in the mathematics classroom in a number of ways: first, you might try and develop algebraic reasoning by asking the pupils what happens to V_t as m increases, or as A decreases. Second, you could extract formal proportional relationships from this formula, such as $m \propto V_t^2$. Both of these approaches could lead to a fuller appreciation of the physical situation. Finally, you could use this formula as an opportunity to practice substituting in values, simplifying the equation if necessary ($g = 9.8\,ms^{-2}$, so the numerator can be rewritten as $19.8m$; you can also make assumptions that turn ρ and C_d into fixed values). Physics contains a huge range of equations in fields as diverse as fluid mechanics and astronomy, and it is worthwhile bringing some of these into the mathematics classroom.

■ The fields of waves and acoustics can provide a visual stimulus for the study of trigonometric graphs. When pupils are taught about longitudinal and transverse wave forms they often fail to connect what they are seeing with the mathematical functions of sine and cosine, and it is worth making these connections explicit. You might choose to bring an oscilloscope into the mathematics classroom (or download an oscilloscope program from the Internet) and challenge pupils to create a 'pure' sine wave with their voice, or any instruments they may have to hand. You could then go on to use ICT to demonstrate the more complicated wave forms that can be made by adding together sine waves with different amplitudes and wavelengths. At a more complex level, oscilloscopes can also demonstrate Lissajous figures, parametric trigonometric curves that represent complex harmonic motion.

- Finally, it is important to recognise that there is some content overlap between the mathematics and physics curricula, and that topics such as distance-time and velocity-time graphs are taught in both subjects. Adopting a physics-aware viewpoint can help pupils to ground these graphs more firmly in real life and identify any simplifications and assumptions that might have been made. These graphs also naturally give rise to the idea of a rate of change, and in this way physics can provide many contexts where the tools of differentiation and integration can be applied. This approach is recognised in some of the A-level mechanics modules.

All three science subjects offer a plethora of contexts within which mathematics can be utilised and explored. If the context used is relevant and authentic its inclusion can benefit both subjects. It can also create an opportunity for pupils to critically appraise the usefulness and accuracy of mathematics in a real-life situation. In this way this kind of cross-curricular activity can develop the broader skill of mathematical modelling, which is discussed further in Chapter 7.

Practical task

Select one of the contexts offered above, or another of your own choice drawn from a science subject. (You might want to look over the science programmes of study (QCA 2007: 206–225) for ideas.) Try to sketch out an idea of how you might use your chosen context in a mathematics lesson.

You might find it useful to ask yourself the following questions as a guide:

- What mathematical concepts or skills does this context develop? Does this make it particularly appropriate for any age group or ability group?

- Does this context rely on any pre-existing knowledge of science? Is there any subject-specific vocabulary I might need to introduce or define? Do I need to check my own understanding with a colleague?

- How might I integrate this context into a lesson: as part of a starter activity, as a main activity, or as part of a plenary?

- What extra equipment could help present this context? Do I need any practical apparatus or pre-prepared ICT resources?

- Are there any possible problems or limitations with using this context? How could I balance these out in the design of the rest of the lesson?

- Does this activity synthesise knowledge, skills and understandings from both mathematics and science? Is this an authentic cross-curricular activity? If not, how could I develop it further?

Looking at your sketch, do you think this would be a fruitful cross-curricular activity? If so, you might like to plan it fully and try it out in the classroom.

CASE STUDY: Discovering Mathematics

One school which has taken advantage of the close relationship between mathematics and science is Ninestiles School, Birmingham. In this school, the staff have designed a two-year, accelerated Key Stage 3 based around the idea of 'reality-based learning'. As part of this, some English skills are taught through humanities contexts, and some mathematics skills are taught through science contexts.

In Years 7 and 8, all of the science and some of the mathematics curriculum time has been combined to form the 'Discovery' programme. This programme is made up of projects that each last for approximately one half-term. At the start of each project pupils are introduced to a new scientific topic, beginning with a question such as 'Should you treat bee and wasp stings in the same way?' or 'What do you actually experience through your senses when you go to see a rock concert?' They are then told how they will be assessed at the end of the project, and what the assessment criteria will be.

In one recent project, pupils had to find out about how runners train before running a marathon, and each group had to produce a magazine article and a wall chart to display their findings. In keeping with the 'reality-based' ethos, some of the training data provided was provided by one of the members of staff at the school who had recently trained for the London marathon. Other projects have included a challenge to design a toy to use on the moon, taking into account the different effect of gravity and the lack of air resistance, and a project based around forensic science. This last assignment started with a pupil accused of a crime he did not commit, and the other pupils had to save him from suspension by gathering evidence, forming a profile of the true suspect, and thinking about estimates, errors and uncertainty. (Of course, it turned out in the end that the teacher did it!)

Alex Hughes, the lead teacher of the Discovery curriculum, believes that this real-life approach to teaching mathematics has served to motivate his pupils, saying that 'you can push pupils to get to a higher level than they'd normally approach in their maths lesson. In your maths lesson you build things up in structured steps – but now pupils are more likely to take a jump.' He notes that when the pupils choose their own level of challenge at the start of each project they are now comfortable with aiming high and selecting something that uses skills and techniques that they do not yet know, since they are more confident in themselves as learners.

Through experience, the teachers on the Discovery programme have found that learners need different levels of guidance and support as they work through each project. After some initial problems, they have settled on a two-tier model of mathematical support. More able learners are generally left to direct the project themselves, but can ask for 'master classes' in any mathematical ideas or techniques that are new to them. Less secure learners, however, often have a more directed start to each project. So in the marathon-training example discussed above, higher ability learners might start independently, and then ask for some teaching on velocity-time graphs after a few lessons, whilst lower ability learners would begin together with some lessons on calculating the mean, mode and median from sets of data.

The authentic nature of the contexts means that some tasks have relied on mathematical ideas that are quite advanced. For instance, one project was based around how a human grows from a single cell. Since the quantity of cells involved keeps doubling, the pupils soon had to deal with very large numbers, and this required pupils to move towards using standard form notation. Some pupils met this challenge admirably, but this step did create a problem for learners with a weaker sense of number, and the teachers involved had to think carefully about how to assess each group's work on its relative merits. In some projects the teachers have found it challenging to factor in mathematics that is authentic and relevant at every level of ability.

On the whole, however, the teachers at Ninestiles are very happy with the way that 'reality-based learning' is serving to challenge and motivate their pupils. Using mathematics to explore and explain questions such as 'how do fireworks work?' has led to pupils developing a more positive view of mathematics, as well as a new view of themselves as active learners.

Practical concerns

The example in the case study above is inspiring, but unfortunately in most schools mathematics and science are taught in a very discrete way. In her research into the use of mathematics in Key Stage 3 science classes Brodsky (2008) reported that there was 'a distinct separation of mathematics and science' (p. 7). This separation did not result from any large philosophical differences, but instead from a lack of communication which led to differences in style, timing and terminology. The teachers that she interviewed 'acknowledged that these inconsistencies created potential barriers to understanding between maths and science for their students' (ibid.). With this in mind, even though the use of science-based examples in mathematics can have many benefits, any overlap in content needs to be handled carefully to ensure that the learners have the best possible cross-curricular experience.

One of the first practical issues to address is that of terminology. Sometimes mathematicians and scientists use different terms for the same idea, such as 'standard form' and 'scientific notation'. On occasion this can lead pupils to think that 'standard form' refers to the number written out in full – in other words, using standard notation. Since the difference in terminology is sometimes imposed by curricula, examination boards and text books in the two subjects, it is impossible to insist on one term or the other. Instead, it would be beneficial for both subjects to acknowledge the existence of the other term. However, it is worth recognising that there is a danger of compartmentalising subjects further by using phrases such as 'this is how we do it in mathematics'. Similar interdepartmental inconsistencies could include the way that graphs are plotted and labelled in each subject, and whether teachers use notation of the form m/s or ms^{-1} for compound units.

A more serious issue arises when mathematicians use terms in an informal, incorrect way which would be frowned upon in physics. Wellington and Ireson (2008) point out that teachers often interchange 'speed' and 'velocity' (as in 'speed-time graphs') and 'mass' and 'weight' (as in 'which unit would you use to measure the weight of this pencil?') Although some instances of these transpositions are clearly more serious than others, and some slips are inevitable given the use of these words in everyday speech, it is still a matter for the mathematics teacher to be aware of. Brodsky (2008) provides some evidence that when science and mathematics teachers do use terms and symbols in a common way, such as the equation $y = mx + c$ to represent a generalised line graph, this can help pupils (p. 8).

Another practical concern is that pupils may encounter topics at different points in each curriculum. One key example is the use of lines of best fit. Whilst lines of best fit are not mentioned explicitly in the science attainment targets until level 7, pupils working at level 5 in science are required to record data, plot it as a graph and look for patterns. This naturally leads to the idea of a line of best fit, and hence in science many pupils are expected to use a line of best fit from the very beginning of Key Stage 3. Conversely, in mathematics the idea is not properly introduced until pupils meet the idea of correlation when they are working at level 6. In science pupils may also encounter the idea of a curve of best fit if it arises naturally from an experimental situation, whereas this idea only features at the very top end of GCSE mathematics syllabuses.

The same problem can occur at higher levels of study. Some pupils encounter inferential statistical tests in science before they meet them in mathematics. Candidates taking A-level biology use tests including Pearson's chi-square test and the Mann-Whitney U test, but these are only introduced in advanced A-level statistics modules, which the majority of A-level mathematics candidates never take. Again, there is no easy solution to this problem, but it is important that each department is aware of possible discrepancies and that teachers do not assume that pupils have already met a concept in another subject without checking. On the other hand, if the pupils have already met a mathematical concept in some guise in science, the mathematics teacher could remind the pupils of this in order to help them make connections and facilitate learning.

The discussion so far has centred on scientific contexts that can be used to illustrate mathematical concepts and techniques. However, the close relationship between mathematics and the sciences offers another way of approaching cross-curricular activity. Instead of focusing on content, the next part of this chapter will consider the skills and processes which link the two subjects.

Cross-curricular processes and the issue of transfer

It is well known that science lessons regularly draw on skills and techniques which are also located within the mathematics curriculum. The old Key Stage 3 national strategy framework document held that:

> Almost every scientific investigation or experiment is likely to require one or more of the mathematical skills of classifying, counting, measuring, calculating, estimating

and recording in tables and graphs. Pupils will, for example, order numbers, including decimals, calculate means and percentages, use negative numbers when taking temperatures, decide whether it is more appropriate to use a line graph or bar chart, and plot, interpret and predict from graphs. They will explore rates of change in cooling curves and distance-time graphs, apply formulae and solve equations, for example, in problems on moments.

(DfEE 2001: 24)

To take advantage of this overlap, however, we require that pupils are able to use skills that they have learnt in one subject in another. This ability to repeat a skill or behaviour in a new situation is known as *transfer*, and is a major area of study in both education and wider psychology.

One way of analysing the act of transfer is to focus on the situations concerned. In this instance it is useful to distinguish between two types of transfer:

Near transfer is to situations that are identical except for a few important differences. A person learns to draw a three-inch line and returns 2 weeks later to learn to draw a five-inch line. Any advantage in learning to draw a five-inch line could be attributed to near transfer from learning to draw a three-inch line. On the other hand, if a person in a list-learning experiment memorized a poem faster because of participation in the list-learning experiment, the transfer would be called far transfer.

(Detterman 1993: 4–5)

If we consider these two types of transfer as lying at opposite ends of a spectrum from 'near' to 'far', then it is fair to suppose that the 'nearer' the situations that transfer is required in, the smaller the cognitive demand that is exerted on the learner. This has practical implications for schools, and explains why some departments attempt to synchronise their curricula. This idea would also argue that transfer becomes more challenging when skills are taught with inconsistencies between departments. Are pupils able to see the graphs of fictitious data that they draw on squared paper in mathematics as being the same as the graphs of experimental data that they draw on graph paper in science? Can the word equations of science be manipulated and rearranged in a similar manner to the equations of arbitrary letters that they have met previously in mathematics? Adopting a measure of consistency, or at least recognising differences explicitly can help to alleviate some of the cognitive demand and encourage pupils to make connections.

The next section of this chapter goes on to look at the experimental evidence that exists concerning transfer, and asks what we might learn from it. However, in order to do this, it is necessary to consider explicitly what is meant by terms such as 'knowledge', 'understanding' and 'learning'.

Over time, psychologists have produced a number of different theories which conceptualise the act of learning, and each theory offers a different perspective on the nature of transfer and poses different challenges to the cross-curricular practitioner. Three of the most important theories in this regard are behaviourism, constructivism and situated cognition.

Behaviourism

The theory of behaviourism holds that the act of learning is based around a series of stimulus-response mechanisms; as such, education can be considered as the process of training a learner to respond in particular ways to a set of recognised prompts. For instance, whenever they hear the prompt 'three times five', many learners display an apparently automatic response of 'fifteen'. Viewing learning in this way allows psychologists to pose and test questions about learning in an empirical way, and does not require the researcher to posit the existence of any hypothetical mental state.

The behaviourist psychologist Edward Thorndike describes a mechanistic approach to teaching and learning mathematics in his books *The Psychology of Arithmetic* (1922) and *The Psychology of Algebra* (1923). In these books he puts forward a law of exercise, which says that connections between the stimulus and response are strengthened as they are used, and a law of effect, which says that responses that lead to positive outcomes and feedback are also strengthened. This view of mathematical learning has been influential in the widespread of rote and practice methods, such as those used in the memorisation of multiplication tables. Some learners have also been seen to develop an automated response to more advanced mathematical topics: for example, upon seeing a trigonometry question, many learners have been trained to label the sides of the triangle, then to select the appropriate ratio, and follow a standard learned set of procedures to reach the answer.

Behaviourism understands transfer as a phenomenon that can occur when situations possess a sufficient degree of commonality in their stimuli; if you set a learner two problems that look sufficiently similar, then they will recognise the similarities and respond appropriately. Whilst there is some disagreement about the interpretation of experimental evidence regarding transfer, studies do seem to support this idea in a broad sense. The research suggests that transfer is both uncommon and difficult, but when it does happen it occurs between situations which are very similar (Detterman 1993). One immediate implication of this for cross-curricular practice is that teachers should strive for consistency in the way different subjects present similar tasks (as discussed above) and actively direct pupils' attention to instances where transfer is being called for.

The difficulty of even near transfer can be perceived in mathematics lessons, when pupils are able to answer questions on a topic if they are worded in a certain way, but are unable to tackle questions that are differently phrased or structured. Catrambone and Holyoak (1990) investigated pupils' ability to solve probability problems and found little evidence of transfer when pupils had previously been trained on questions centred on a specific subgoal. They suggested that teachers should therefore give pupils practice on questions phrased in a variety of ways. Reed *et al.* (1985) also found limited evidence of transfer when investigating how pupils fared solving algebra word problems. Surprisingly, when pupils had a solution to a problem in front of them their ability to solve equivalent problems improved, but their ability to solve problems that were only similar did not improve.

Bassok and Holyoak (1993) found evidence of different degrees of transfer between different combinations of subjects, and also an asymmetry in the direction of transfer. In one experiment they investigated pupils' performances in problems in algebra and physics that were structurally isomorphic; for example, a question on arithmetic progressions could be mapped to a question about the motion of a vehicle travelling with constant acceleration in a straight line. They found that it was more common for pupils to transfer skills from algebra to physics than vice versa. In another experiment they constructed similar problems in algebra and finance, and observed a greater degree of transfer than had been the case between algebra and physics.

Reflective task

To what extent do you think that learning mathematics can be described as responding to stimuli? In what ways might a learner be trained to think in a more cross-curricular way? Do you think that transfer is a learnt skill?

Although the results discussed above can be understood in terms of situations with different levels of similarity in their stimuli, another possibility is that the pupils had built up their understandings in a way that made transfer to algebra a qualitatively different task for learners who had studied finance compared to those who had studied physics. This shift of focus from the situation to the learners themselves requires a different theory of learning.

Constructivism

Constructivism is a theory of learning that is concerned primarily with what might be going on inside the mind of the learner. As such, it requires researchers to consider mental constructions and operations that express themselves through pupils' actions but are not directly examinable.

There are a number of significantly different schools of constructivist thought, but most are built around two key principles:

- knowledge is not passively received but built up by the cognizing subject
- the function of cognition is adaptive and serves the organization of the experiential world, not the discovery of ontological reality

(von Glasersfeld 1995: 18)

The first of these principles states that we should not view pupils as passive vessels to whom knowledge can be transmitted, but instead as active learners who construct their own knowledge through perception, experience and independent thought. The second principle suggests that each learner builds up a unique understanding of a concept which may be subtly different from the understandings of those around them. However, as long as it can make sense of their experiences of that concept it is sufficient, as building knowledge is about constructing something that works when it is needed, rather than striving for an independently existing and objective truth.

Together these principles are radical in their scope, as they allow us to consider whether learners might construct knowledge in different ways. They also allow us to ask whether these different processes of construction can lead to qualitatively different forms of knowledge or understanding. Skemp (1976), for instance, suggests that learners can build an 'understanding' of something in two different ways. *Instrumental* understanding consists of 'rules without reasons', whereas *relational* understanding is made up of an appreciation of what to do in a situation and why. Each type of understanding has advantages and disadvantages: whilst instrumental understanding is quicker to build it is often less flexible; relational understanding might incur a greater cognitive demand but it is usually more adaptable to new problems and often more memorable as well.

Hiebert and Lefevre (1986) drew a similar distinction between *procedural* and *conceptual* forms of knowledge. In mathematics, procedural knowledge is made up of the algorithms or rules of a technique, together with information about the requisite symbols or language. Conceptual knowledge, on the other hand, can include knowledge about how and why a method works, its limitations and its connections with other mathematical ideas:

> Conceptual knowledge is characterized most clearly as knowledge that is rich in relationships. It can be thought of as a connected web of knowledge, a network in which the linking relationships are as prominent as the discrete pieces of information.
>
> (Hiebert and Lefevre 1986: 3–4)

Research suggests that conceptual knowledge tends to lead to more flexible problem-solving and a higher degree of transfer within mathematics (Rittle-Johnson and Alibabi 1999). It would also appear to promote transfer between mathematics and other subjects. Zakaria (2004) researched the different ways in which students appeared to transfer their knowledge across the boundaries between mathematics and chemistry. She found that students who seemed to develop mainly procedural knowledge were more likely to perceive the two subjects as separate and disconnected. On the other hand, students who seemed to develop conceptual knowledge had stronger inter-network links and were able to transfer knowledge more effectively. Transfer then, whilst difficult, can be helped to develop if pupils are encouraged to build up conceptual knowledge of mathematical ideas.

A constructivist interpretation of the finding of Bassok and Holyoak (1993), that students found it harder to transfer skills from physics to mathematics than from mathematics to physics, could follow a similar argument. If skills are initially encountered in physics, embedded in a particular context, then a learner might construct primarily procedural knowledge when practising this type of problem. However, if skills are introduced abstractly in mathematics lessons and then shown to have relevance in a large variety of contexts, then the learner might be more likely to see relationships and connections from the beginning, and hence develop conceptual knowledge.

Another intriguing possibility raised by the work of Bassok and Holyoak is that it might be easier for pupils to move between finance and mathematics than between physics and mathematics, because finance and mathematics use similar forms of concepts. The concepts used in mathematics and finance are typically static and discrete, whereas the concepts used in physics are often dynamic and continuous. If moving between different types of ideas does add another layer of difficulty, then a teacher would need to consider this when choosing which examples to use, and be mindful of the psychological constructions of their pupils.

> ## Reflective task
>
> Think of two or three contexts that might be used to motivate pupils to study decimals in a mathematics lesson. To what extent do you think each context would challenge a pupil to think about what they were doing? How much do you think each context would challenge a pupil to make links with other ideas and topics? Do you think all contexts develop pupils' understanding in the same way?

Situated cognition

Situated cognition is an alternative theory of learning which sits in stark contrast to both behaviourism and constructivism. It holds that the act of knowing cannot be separated from the act of doing; knowledge is situated in activity, which is bound to social and cultural contexts. Knowledge is no longer seen as something which can be stored and retrieved by an individual, but as something which occurs *in situ*. 'Learning' means improving at performing an activity or action.

This idea is supported by the work on 'street mathematics' carried out by Nunes *et al.* (1993). In their work they found that people's mathematical performance often depends on whether they are in school or in a real-life situation. For instance, street vendors in Brazil were successful at performing arithmetic as a real-life skill, and comfortably used concepts such as proportionality and inverse operations on the street. However, they did not manage to perform as well in school-based tests. A similar study was performed by Lave (1988) who demonstrated that adults used different mathematical strategies in the supermarket than they did at home. The nature of mathematics used by many learners appears to be qualitatively different depending on the situation and circumstances.

This perspective gives rise to some difficult questions. The focused objectives of classroom tasks often lead teachers to strip activities of superficial details and features which are not deemed relevant. However, it may be these very features which make the task authentic and the learning meaningful. Is it possible that school mathematics departments are merely teaching learners how to succeed at their own, situated version of mathematics that will ultimately offer little support to pupils in the real-world?

> School activity too often tends to be hybrid, implicitly framed by one culture, but explicitly attributed to another. Classroom activity very much takes place within the culture of schools, although it is attributed to the culture of readers, writers, mathematicians, historians, economists, geographers, and so forth. Many of the activities students undertake are simply not the activities of practitioners and would not make sense or be endorsed by the cultures to which they are attributed. This hybrid activity, furthermore, limits students' access to the important structuring and supporting cues that arise from the context. What students do tends to be ersatz activity.
>
> (J.S. Brown *et al.* 1989: 34)

The idea of transfer has been understood in a number of ways by researchers who hold to the theory of situated cognition, but it essentially involves the recognition of invariant elements through the ability to rearrange and reconsider different situations. In many ways this idea echoes the practice recommended by the behaviourist understanding of transfer; consistency in the details and presentation of problems across subjects could improve the potential for transfer.

The theory of situated cognition is challenging in a number of respects. However, it can be seen as offering a theoretical basis of support for cross-curricular activity that strives for authenticity in its presentation and design. In particular it resonates with many of the ideas of work-based learning, and the expansion of the idea of schooling to include apprenticeships, mentoring and the introduction of experts and real-life practitioners into the classroom.

Reflective task

Consider the mathematics that your pupils might perform informally throughout the day. Do you think that they always recognise what they are doing as mathematics? Do you feel that there is a qualitative difference between the mathematics pupils do in the classroom and the mathematics that pupils use outside of school?

Each theory of learning views transfer in a different way and raises different questions that need to be considered when designing cross-curricular practice. The key issues can be summarised as follows:

- **Transfer is difficult and cannot be assumed.** It is inappropriate to assume that if a pupil can complete a task in one subject then they have mastery over the associated skill in all contexts. The difficulty inherent in transfer can be tempered by presenting situations in a more consistent way and pointing out instances of transfer to pupils.

- **Fuller understanding makes transfer more likely.** If pupils have learnt to recognise, or have built up an understanding of the relationships between different ideas and concepts, then they are more likely to be able to apply their knowledge in a new situation. Rote-learning and domain-specific techniques can lead to less flexibility in thinking.

- **Abstract and context-based learning must be held in balance.** Both of these types of learning are required at different stages if pupils are to develop the skills needed for transfer. In particular, it is valuable for a learner to be exposed to a range of contexts that use an abstract skill in qualitatively different ways, and for learners to make cross-curricular links between a range of subjects and concepts.

- **Transfer can be developed through challenge and metacognition.** It is helpful for pupils to identify instances of transfer when they occur, and to develop recognition of the skills they are using. However, this level of reflection is unlikely to grow if they only encounter trivial instances of transfer, and so a range of difficulties is beneficial. Authentic, open cross-curricular challenges can help to provide this range.

■ **Transfer is a key skill for pupils if they are to apply their learning in the 'real world'.** If pupils' learning is to be of any worth when they leave school they will have to be able to adapt it appropriately to new situations. It is also possible to suggest that all learning is some form of transfer, in which case the development of the skill of transfer is a fundamental aim of schooling.

Practical planning for transfer

One skill that is used in both mathematics and science is the skill of being able to rearrange an equation into a more convenient form. The cognitive processes that algebra can involve are many and complicated, but the points above give rise to some suggestions about how this particular topic might be covered in the mathematics classroom to promote transfer. These suggestions are not exhaustive or suitable for every class, but you might like to consider whether you would use variations of these strategies in your own teaching.

First, it would be useful for pupils to be told expressly that they are developing a skill that is used in other subjects, particularly science. Ironically, some GCSE mathematics textbooks use equations from science (such as $V = IR$) for practice purposes but do not tell the reader where they have come from. As a mathematics teacher you might like to find five or six equations that pupils have previously encountered in science and use them as examples; alternatively, you could challenge pupils in advance to research some examples themselves and bring them in to the lesson.

Second, it would be helpful to pupils if different approaches to rearranging equations were addressed. This would most likely include the rearrangement of word equations, rearranging equations expressed in symbols, and using a 'formula triangle' for equations such as speed = distance ÷ time. Pupils would be encouraged to spot that the methods are largely equivalent, and this might perhaps lead into some discussion on the strengths and weaknesses of each method. In addition to this, it would be advantageous to find out in advance from the science department which of these methods they commonly use.

Third, you might use resources from the science department in the mathematics classroom to reaffirm the notion that it is the same skill being used in both situations. Although it might seem trivial to the teacher, swapping a mathematics textbook for a science textbook for part of a lesson is a strongly symbolic gesture to a pupil. Inviting a science teacher into the mathematics classroom would have a similar impact. Finally, it would be beneficial to the pupils to arrange some form of follow-up. You might be able to arrange it so that the pupils' next science lesson uses the skills that the pupils have just learnt in mathematics; if this lesson utilised some of the same equations as well then the process of transfer would be even clearer to the pupils.

Practical task

Another skill used in both mathematics and science is the interpretation of real-life graphs. Using the theoretical discussion above and the example provided, suggest some ways in which you might teach this in mathematics so as to promote transfer.

Summary

Of all the subjects in the school curriculum, mathematics and science have a distinctively close relationship. To the mathematics teacher, science offers a cornucopia of contexts. Sometimes a context shows how mathematical ideas can be used, such as when proportion is used to express relationships in chemical kinetics. On other occasions the scientific context provides a good physical picture of an abstract idea; the use of the quadrat in ecology is a powerful illustration of the idea of random sampling.

However, the association between the two subjects is more profound than that, and often mathematics teachers and science teachers find themselves teaching the same skills, and sometimes even the same content. This offers both departments an exceptional first step towards cross-curricular provision. If departments communicate regularly, recognise the content of each others' syllabuses and commit to making connections, the potential for cross-curricular learning is extraordinary, both within regular lessons and as part of broader cross-curricular projects.

Professional Standards for QTS

This chapter will help you meet the following Q standards: Q6, Q8, Q10, Q14.

Professional Standards for Teachers

This chapter will help you meet the following core standards: C6, C8, C10, C15.

Further reading

QCA (2007) *The National Curriculum 2007 Science Programmes of Study* (pp. 206–225).
It is worthwhile familiarising yourself with the scope and nature of the programmes of study for science. Browse through them and look for instances where you feel mathematics is explicitly referenced, and places where you feel cross-curricular approaches to teaching could bolster pupils' understanding of a topic or skill.
Skemp, R.R. (1976) 'Instrumental Understanding and Relational Understanding', *Mathematics Teaching*, 77: 20–26.
This short and popular article contains a number of profound ideas about the different ways that people claim to 'understand' things. It has a great deal of relevance for anyone involved in teaching or learning mathematics.

4

Construction and feedback: mathematics and technology

If you were to think of mathematics and science as sibling subjects, then mathematics and technology would be close cousins. Although different secondary schools focus on different strands of technology in their provision, in every strand pupils work to combine theoretical ideas with creative thinking and practical skills to design and produce products. Mathematics serves as a vital part of this process, providing a language and means with which pupils can learn about and explore underlying structures and relationships in the physical world.

In return, technology offers a lot to the mathematics teacher. Not only does the technology curriculum contain a number of mathematics-rich contexts, but ideas and equipment from technology can allow pupils to create physical products in the classroom for themselves. This act of construction has a number of benefits: it is motivating, it can promote a sense of personal ownership of the ideas used, and it may even lead to learners constructing a qualitatively better understanding of the underlying mathematics.

This chapter explores how physically creating a product can motivate and develop learners' mathematical understanding, and examines a theory of learning, constructionism, which may account for this phenomenon. It also offers a number of examples of cross-curricular connections between the two subject areas, including a case study of a teacher who has embraced the potential of technology and introduced robots into his mathematics classroom.

Key objectives

By the end of this chapter, you will have:

- Explored some of the links between the secondary mathematics curriculum and the curricula of the technology subjects
- Considered how the creation of a physical product can act as a motivator, a feedback provider and a source of further challenge
- Met another theory of learning, constructionism, and seen how some of its principles encourage the introduction of technology into the mathematics classroom

- Thought about some of the practical issues associated with using physical equipment in the mathematics classroom

- Encountered a number of cross-curricular activities linking mathematics and technology, and started devising some of your own

The place of technology in secondary schools

The 2008 National Curriculum (QCA 2007) lays out a statutory curriculum for design and technology at Key Stage 3, which includes content organised under the subheadings of designing, food, resistant materials, textiles, and systems and control. However, unlike mathematics and science, there is no statutory programme of study at Key Stage 4, and so schools differ significantly in their provision. Exam boards offer a variety of qualifications under the banner of 'technology'. These include GCSEs based around graphic design, electronics and each of the subheadings used at Key Stage 3.

There are many other qualifications that can be considered as 'technology', ranging from short courses in general design and technology to diplomas in engineering and construction and the built environment. The examples and discussion in this chapter are designed to be relevant for all such qualifications, but if you are currently working in a school, it is important to find out about the technology department's current provision before starting to work on any extensive cross-curricular plans.

Methods in technology

It is readily apparent that technology utilises a wide range of basic mathematical skills, such as measuring, estimating and calculating. Particular emphases include selecting and using appropriate units in a range of contexts, and dealing with tolerances. Looking beyond this, however, it is interesting to draw some parallels between how a pupil might solve a problem in a mathematics lesson, and how they might approach a task in technology. For example, consider the stages of the data–handling cycle: specify the problem, collect the data, process the data, interpret and evaluate the data. Now compare these with the stages that a pupil goes through when designing a product to solve a problem or meet a particular purpose.

> An important application of mathematics is its role in the solving of problems. Many authors have given an explanation of the role of mathematics in the process of problem solving in terms of a cycle … This mirrors the way in which a child might work through a design and make assignment. He/she will not necessarily go through each stage in a linear or a cyclical path. The process will almost certainly be iterative.
>
> (DATA 2008)

This overlap can be also seen in the 'key concepts' and the 'key processes' sections of the two subjects in the National Curriculum. Whilst the discussion in this chapter will mainly consider potential cross-curricular contexts, it is also valuable to encourage pupils to reflect on their work in the two subjects in a metacognitive way, and to point out to them how the value of proper planning, evaluation and iterative working is recognised in many disciplines.

Technology contexts for mathematics

As with science, there are hundreds of possible contexts that could be used in the mathematics classroom to demonstrate the use and value of different concepts and techniques. Previous chapters have already mentioned the use of gears to exemplify the topic of ratio, and shown how electronic engineers must add fractions to calculate the combined resistance of two resistors connected in parallel. Further examples are offered below to illustrate six of the most common areas of technology studied in secondary schools.

Food technology

Mathematics offers a range of tools which allow pupils to undertake quantitative comparisons between different types of food and assess their nutritional value. For instance, a pupil might research the amount of protein, carbohydrate, sugar, fat and fibre in 30 g servings of five different breakfast cereals and present their results using composite bar charts.

The issue of healthy eating and the construction of a healthy diet plan can be approached at many levels of difficulty. At the most basic level pupils can consider, compare and add the calorific values of different foods. A more complicated exercise would be to present pupils with a range of nutritional information panels (or the briefer 'traffic lights' summaries often found on packaging) and challenge them to find combinations of foodstuffs that offered the right amount of calories, fat, protein and carbohydrate for different groups of people in society.

A more challenging activity for A-level pupils is detailed in Toumasis (2004). In this article, the writer describes how to construct a simple model of weight loss using first-order differential equations. This model leads to an asymptotic graph of weight loss which pupils could discuss and compare to real-life experience. Pupils might like to go on to critically challenge and refine the model. The topic of a balanced diet occurs in a number of curriculum areas; in this way an authentic cross-curricular approach will also draw on skills and understandings from science and PSHCE.

Other potential contexts from food technology include scaling recipes, designing and using questionnaires to evaluate products, and using the principles of critical path analysis to plan and cook meals.

Graphics

A lot of the overlap between mathematics and graphics occurs in the field of technical drawing. Graphics qualifications tend to require pupils to communicate their designs and ideas effectively, and this often requires drawing skills. However, it is worth noting that the increasing availability of technology means that some pupils will focus on computer-generated representations (although this involves some behind-the-scenes mathematics of its own).

Pupils studying graphical design should be able to appreciate the worth of learning constructions such as the perpendicular bisector, angle bisector and the equilateral triangle. A related exercise would be to challenge the pupils to construct a half-protractor that goes up in increments of 15° using only a straight-edge and a pair of compasses. However, you might like to go beyond the mathematics syllabus to consider shapes such as ellipses.

There are a number of ways to construct an ellipse. One way is to start with a straight line AB, where the points A and B are the foci of the ellipse. Attach the ends of a piece of string that is longer than AB to the foci. Now place a pen underneath the string and stretch it until it is taut. Move the pen around, keeping the string taut, and you will have drawn an ellipse. This method draws an entire ellipse, but it is not immediately obvious how to use it to construct an ellipse of a particular size. It is within the scope of A-level students to consider the geometry behind this method, and relate it to the special case that occurs when the two foci merge, and the ellipse becomes a circle.

An alternative method (shown in Figure 4.1) is to draw a major circle (using the major axis of the ellipse as the diameter) and a minor circle (using the minor axis of the ellipse as a diameter) using the same point as the centre of both circles. Now draw in between four and six diagonal lines that go through this centre. Wherever a diagonal hits the minor circle, draw a small vertical line, and wherever a diagonal hits the major circle, draw a small horizontal line. Mark the points where the vertical and horizontal lines from each diagonal meet, then join them to form an ellipse. Again, this method can be justified in a neat way by A-level students and leads to a nice use of the parametric form of the equation of an ellipse.

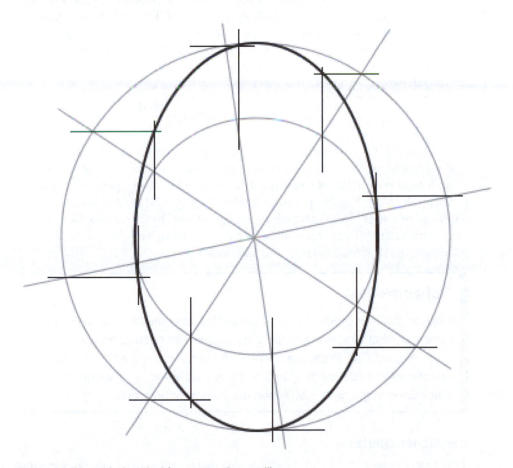

Figure 4.1 A graphical method for constructing an ellipse.

Other links between the two subjects include 2-D representations of 3-D objects through plans and elevations; isometric drawing of 3-D shapes (and in graphics, planometric and axonometric drawing as well); and scale drawing and modelling.

Product design

The product design strand of technology requires pupils to be familiar with a number of mathematical aspects of industrial practice. This includes logistical techniques such as 'just in time' delivery systems which relate to ideas from decision mathematics, and quality control procedures which are underpinned by statistics. Commercial and industrial applications such as these provide a fertile source of contexts for use in the mathematics classroom.

In addition, mathematics can be shown to play a role in the design of the product itself. This idea is taken up by the popular economics writer Robert Frank, who attempts to explain why milk is often sold in (near) rectangular containers, whilst soft drinks are sold in cylindrical ones. He proposes that milk tends to be kept in the fridges of convenience stores, which have limited space; therefore it is important to use a shape that tessellates. Soft drinks, however, are kept on the shelf, and need to be easy to hold and carry, so a circular cross-section is perhaps more appropriate (Frank 2007: 21–24).

Even if we adopt the shape of a cylinder, we are still left with the question of which cylinder would minimise waste, a principle of design taught in technology classes. This too can be addressed using mathematics; if the volume ($\pi r^2 h$) is fixed at 330 cm³, the modal volume for a carbonated beverage, we can rearrange the formula for the surface area as follows:

$$SA = 2\pi r^2 + 2\pi rh = 2\pi r^2 + \frac{660}{r}$$

Differentiating this with respect to r gives the optimal radius of 3.74 cm, and leads to an optimal height of 7.49 cm. This is close to what is seen in practice, but not exactly right; to understand why this is the case pupils might need to investigate the historical design of the product, or consider bringing in understanding from another subject, psychology. They might also go on to compare the design of soft drinks cans to the taller, thinner cylinders often used by energy drinks companies, and weigh up the sometimes competing influences of environmental concerns and branding.

Reflective task

Choose another product which you think pupils might know well, and consider what factors went into the design of its packaging and presentation. Can mathematics be used to assess the efficiency and effectiveness of the packaging? Beyond mathematics, what other disciplines might have influenced the design of the packaging?

Resistant materials

This strand requires pupils to develop a knowledge and understanding of the materials and technologies used in the manufacture of different products. It often uses basic numerical comparisons when pupils have to compare the physical qualities of two different materials, or when they investigate the make-up and characteristics of composite materials such as reinforced concrete.

One exciting modern context in this area is the study of geodesic structures. These are lattice shell structures mapped out by great circles that intersect to form triangular elements. The major advantage of such structures is that they require no internal supports, and since they are generally part-spheres they tend towards maximising the enclosed volume for a given surface area. Perhaps the most famous example of a geodesic structure is the AT&T Pavilion at Epcot in Disney World.

It is possible to get pupils to construct a half-dome themselves in the mathematics classroom, and there are many sites on the Internet that offer instructions on how to do this. Two possibilities are to get the class to work as a whole and make the structure out of rolled up newspaper, or to get them working in small groups with cocktail sticks and soft pastille sweets. This kind of activity offers a number of opportunities in terms of the PLTS discussed in Chapter 1, and also results in a physical model that the pupils can inspect and test for strength.

Questions that can be asked to explore the mathematics involved include: what types of triangles make up the structure? What polygons do the triangles make up? Why would it be impossible to create a dome just using two dimensional regular hexagons? (This last question also helps to explain the shape of a football.) Pupils might go on to explore more three dimensional geometry, looking at Platonic solids such as the icosahedron.

Questions that can be asked to explore the technology include: why is a triangle such a strong shape in construction? How does the geometry of the dome serve to balance the forces of tension and compression? What is meant by 'tensegrity'? What construction and planning issues might be problematic when trying to turn a dome into a living space?

The benefits that arise out of the pupils creating a physical product are discussed in more detail below.

Systems and control

Electrical circuits and their components follow a number of rules that can be expressed algebraically, most famously Ohm's Law ($I = V \div R$) which states that if the temperature remains constant the current (I) through a conductor joining two points is proportional to the voltage (V) across the two points and inversely proportional to the resistance (R) between them. As was discussed in the previous chapter with regard to science, these kinds of relationships allow pupils to explore the idea of proportionality and practice rearranging equations and substituting in values. The physical context allows the pupils to consider the physical implications of their answers, and evaluate their meaning. Other sources of equations within this strand of technology include hydraulics and pneumatics.

At a higher level, the study of electronics requires more advanced mathematics, such as the use of differential equations to model the charge and discharge of a capacitor. At this point the issue of transfer becomes even more pronounced. Waks (1988) conducted a teaching experiment with two groups of 17–18 year old students studying electronics. The treatment group experienced a period of connected teaching, where the content, teaching strategies and timings were co-ordinated between the mathematics and technology departments. This group achieved significantly higher scores on average than the control group, who experienced regular teaching from both departments. Moreover, the answers of the treatment group appeared to demonstrate a greater degree of conceptual knowledge as opposed to procedural knowledge, echoing the findings of Zakaria (2004) and the discussion of the previous chapter. The issue of transfer, then, is as relevant in technology as it is in science.

Another aspect of systems and control that links strongly to mathematics is the topic of truth tables, which comes to electronics from the field of propositional logic. In electronics, a truth table is a table of values that gives the output of a logic circuit for every possible combination of two inputs. So using 0 to represent false and 1 to represent true, the truth tables of the 'AND' and 'OR' gates with two inputs, A and B are:

AND gate

A	B	Output
0	0	0
0	1	0
1	0	0
1	1	1

OR gate

A	B	Output
0	0	0
0	1	1
1	0	1
1	1	1

Figure 4.2 Truth tables for AND and OR gates.

In the mathematics classroom such truth tables can be used to develop logical thinking, and introduce ideas drawn from logic such as De Morgan's laws.

Textiles

As with 'product design' the textiles industry uses a lot of industrial mathematics, ranging from statistical experiments investigating the variability of different fibres, to the aerodynamics of manufacturing processes and the mechanics and properties of different fabrics. Unfortunately, much of this mathematics lies beyond the scope of the secondary curriculum, but the textiles strand of technology still has much to offer the mathematics classroom.

The National Curriculum for design and technology requires pupils to develop an appreciation for the role of aesthetic elements, and this is key to pupils' success in textiles. Mathematically speaking, this invokes ideas such as symmetry and tessellation. These ideas are frequently observed in the practice of quilting. Quilt designs are often based around geometric shapes and are deliberately constructed so as to possess line and rotational symmetry. Some details on how you might introduce quilting in the classroom are given in Faux and Hepburn (2008); at the time of writing there is also an ATM working group on mathematical quilting which offers ideas, activities and resources at www.atm.org.uk/resources/quilting.html.

Practical task

The contexts discussed in each chapter of this book can be used in a number of different, equally valid ways. As you read through the examples provided it is valuable to actively consider which of the contexts you might seek to include in your own practice, and also how you might do so.

Drawing from either the contexts outlined above or the design and technology section of the National Curriculum (QCA 2007: 50–59) select a technology-based context that you think:

- would promote learning if it were formed the basis of a short activity in a mathematics lesson
- would develop thinking if it was used as the basis of a longer, open-ended task
- would be most effective if it was used within extra-curricular provision, possibly as part of a 'maths club'

Out of the three contexts that you have chosen, do you think there is one that stands out as having the potential to be a productive cross-curricular activity? If so, you might like to plan it fully and try it out in the classroom.

Technology and sustainable development

Before moving on to consider some of the theoretical issues behind the use of technological contexts in the classroom, it is worth noting that 'technology' is a term with a broad range of meanings, and that many of the contexts used above begin to use skills and understandings from additional disciplines. For instance, food technology links to issues of health and well-being; product design can connect to ideas from psychology; and the study of textiles is strongly related to art and design. The wide scope of technology as a discipline establishes it as an important part of many cross-curricular topics that stretch across more than two subjects.

One key example of this comes in the cross-curriculum dimension 'global dimension and sustainable development' (QCA 2007: 'Cross-Curriculum Dimensions' section). This theme seeks to consider and address contemporary issues of a global nature, such as human rights, global poverty, climate change and sustainable development. An understanding of technology is clearly central to any discussion of alternative energy sources, and such discussion is enhanced enormously by the introduction of mathematical tools. It is important for learners to gain a quantitative appreciation of key issues such as the relative efficiency of these technologies and the extent to which they are currently being used. This understanding can then be further developed by considering social issues.

For example, it would be possible to structure a cross-curricular project around wind turbines. The mathematics could initially include the construction of a time series graph to show the increase in wind power over the last thirty years, and some related calculations to discover what percentage of Britain's power is generated by wind turbines.

This could lead onto a discussion of the technology of wind turbines, and an explanation of how the wind turbine converts kinetic energy from the wind into rotational kinetic energy, and then into electrical energy. The mathematical formula for the power in Watts, P, generated by a wind turbine is:

$$P = \frac{1}{2}\rho A v^3 C_p$$

where ρ is the density of air, A is the swept area, v is the wind speed in metres per second, and C_p is a coefficient reflecting the efficiency of the turbine design. This coefficient varies between each design of turbine but has a theoretical maximum (known as the Betz limit) of 0.59.

Possible cross-curricular questions from this point include:

- How is the power of the turbine related to the density of the surrounding air? What factors might alter the density of air, and hence vary the power being produced? (mathematics and science)

- How is the power of the turbine connected to the area swept out by the blades? If the blade length was doubled, what would happen to the power produced by the turbine? (mathematics and technology)

- How is the power of the turbine connected to the wind speed? Given that everything else is held constant, draw a sketch graph of the power output against the wind speed. (mathematics and technology)

- The government decides to place a wind farm somewhere in your county. Using a map and considering the variables in the formula above, choose a location for the wind farm and justify your choice. (mathematics, geography and citizenship)

- Research the design of different types of turbine. What values of C_p are typical? Explain why the wind turbine is not 100 per cent efficient. (mathematics, science and technology)

Each of these questions can be posed as they are, or developed further. In the case of the third question, real-life wind farms are often placed with help from an additional calculated quantity, wind power density, and pupils might wish to investigate this. In the fifth question, the value of C_p actually varies with the wind speed, so an extra layer of mathematical sophistication (and accuracy) can be added on. This involves pupils calculating the tip speed ratio of the blades, which requires them to imagine the locus of the tip of the blade and use the formula for the circumference of a circle.

Alternatively, pupils might go on to consider the economics of wind turbines, and create a financial model using the set-up and running costs of a turbine together with the money made by generating electricity. They could explore the relationship between a turbine's financial viability and the proportion of 'downtime' that a turbine experiences when it is too windy or not windy enough, or compare the economic potential of wind turbines as a power source against that of solar panels. As is often the way with cross-curricular scenarios, there are a multitude of interesting and valid questions that combine the individual subjects in a number of different ways.

The topic of multi-subject cross-curricular opportunities is returned to at various places within this book. The example of wind turbines and renewable power is offered here to demonstrate that technology (and the mathematics contained within it) not only drives smaller, discrete contexts, but also lies at the heart of some of the key issues facing contemporary society.

Physical products in the mathematics classroom

A number of the examples discussed above could be integrated into the mathematics classroom in such a way that the pupils physically make something for themselves. When such manipulable products are created in the classroom, they can contribute to the teaching and learning process in a number of ways. For instance, if a physical product has been created through pupils' explicit use of mathematical ideas and concepts, it can serve as a source of feedback. In the case of the geodesic dome models discussed above, the strength of each dome made serves as an indicator of how accurately pupils have followed the instructions, as well as a testable illustration of the idea of 'tensegrity'. The teacher is no longer the sole source of assessment and feedback, and this can alter the classroom dynamic in a positive way.

One idea that has been used in mathematics classrooms is to use the principle of moments to construct a device that acts as a feedback mechanism. Imagine a balancing beam that has been marked at equal intervals emanating out from the pivot at the centre of the beam. The teacher places a weight of 60 g at a point four marks to the left of the pivot and offers the pupils a weight of 40 g. Where should they place the new weight in order to make the beam return to its original horizontal position? This type of activity can be used to develop multiplication and division skills, or to generate and solve simple algebraic equations. In both cases, however, the question of 'right' or 'wrong' is not addressed by the teacher, but is seen to be a property of the system. The pupils also get a sense of how far away they are from the solution; the nature of the feedback has moved away from a simple 'yes' or 'no' and become something more subtle.

It can be argued that the creation and construction of physical products also brings about a number of affective benefits. Construction activities can be motivating, and the direct involvement of the pupil can lead them to develop a greater sense of ownership over the mathematics, and encourage them to view the subject as a more personal, relevant discipline. The theory of constructionism, however, goes further by suggesting that if pupils explore mathematical concepts using equipment that they can interact with and manipulate, they can develop a qualitatively better form of knowledge.

Reflective task

Think back on your own experiences as a pupil at secondary school. Did you ever use practical equipment as part of a mathematics lesson? Did you ever use practical equipment in other subjects? Do you feel that having something to manipulate and experiment with motivated you? Do you feel that it helped you develop your knowledge, or improved your understanding?

Constructionism

The role and importance of children's interactions with the environment has always been a key area of interest for educational psychologists. The Swiss psychologist Piaget, who is often viewed as the father of child psychology, considered action to be the very basis of thought, stating that 'thought can only replace action on the basis of data which action itself provides' (Piaget and Inhelder 1956: 453).

This perceived dominance of physical actions in the development of knowledge led the mathematician and educator Seymour Papert to develop a theory of learning known as constructionism. This begins with the principles of the theory of constructivism as discussed in the previous chapter, but then stresses the benefits available to a learner who is able to externally construct a related, meaningful object in parallel with their internal construction of knowledge.

> Constructionism--the N word as opposed to the V word--shares constructivism's connotation of learning as "building knowledge structures" irrespective of the circumstances of the learning. It then adds the idea that this happens especially felicitously in a context where the learner is consciously engaged in constructing a public entity, whether it's a sand castle on the beach or a theory of the universe.
>
> (Papert 1991: 1)

Papert was one of the co-creators of the LOGO programming language, which exemplifies many constructionist ideals. There are many forms of LOGO, but the form most commonly seen in schools consists of a cursor or 'turtle' on a computer screen (or a turtle robot on the floor) which draws shapes whilst following commands given to it by a pupil. Typical commands include FD 100 to make the 'turtle' move forward 100 units, and RT 90 to result in a turn of 90 degrees to the right.

In LOGO, pupils have the opportunity to construct something external to themselves which then provides feedback on their own, developing, internal understanding. Papert sees turtle geometry as a computational, dynamic geometry. Pupils can visually explore concepts such as angle and length, then organise and reorganise their thoughts in light of new evidence and experiments. The turtle even allows them to visualise and express theorems in a new way, such as is the case with the total turtle trip theorem: 'If a turtle takes a trip around the boundary of any area and ends up in the state in which it started, then the sum of all turns will be 360 degrees' (Papert 1993: 76). LOGO develops in complexity along with the learner, and commands such as REPEAT and the introduction of user-defined procedures allows for the exploration of mathematical ideas such as symmetry, iteration and recursion, as well as introducing pupils to computer programming.

Whilst LOGO is not used as widely as it used to be, the constructionist ideals that lay behind it can be realised through the use of dynamic geometry software such as Cabri, Geometer's Sketchpad and Geogebra, as well as through visualisation software such as Autograph. The principles of constructionism also provide a highly relevant motivation for cross-curricular projects linking mathematics and technology. One such project is detailed below.

CASE STUDY: Mathematics and Robots

Garry Redrup is a mathematics teacher based in Reading who has utilised a number of constructionist principles in the classroom – by introducing pupils to robots!

It began when Garry came across the Lego ® Mindstorms ® NXT series of equipment and recognised its potential for getting pupils to engage with mathematical ideas. A typical kit from this range will contain a microcomputer block running programmable software, along with three motors, and sensors which detect sound, light, distance and motor rotation. The kit also comes with an array of Lego ® bricks and parts giving the freedom to design the robot to carry out any task. Kits can be customised later by purchasing additional sensors and equipment as required. Together with a colleague, Dr Ashley Green, Garry has developed a number of activities which use this equipment in the classroom.

One such activity centres on the use of an 'automated calliper'. This robot (see Figure 4.3) uses a motor to squeeze two arms either side of a block of MDF. A touch sensor tells the robot when to stop. The robot then reports a numerical value on the display screen showing how far the motor has turned. Pupils can use the automated calliper on pieces of wood with different thicknesses and then begin to ask questions. Will the robot give the same answer each time for wood of the same thickness? Can the pupils guess what the next answer will be? Would a conversion graph serve to translate the reported response in degrees into a thickness in millimetres?

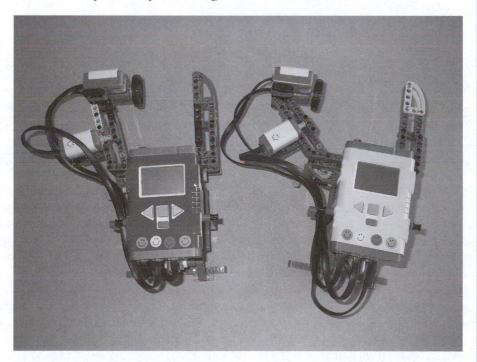

Figure 4.3 Automated calliper robots.

Garry is encouraged by the different questions that such a robot can give rise to: 'it's real-life graphs, it's estimating … it's all sort of things that come up. You can keep revisiting it with different year groups.' For instance, the automated calliper robot exhibits a very small persistent error, which A-level pupils might be able to deduce comes from the fact that the motion of the robot follows an arc, not a straight line.

Once the robots start to become mobile (a design is included in the kit), there are a lot more possibilities as pupils begin to consider how to get robots to move along different loci. For instance, if a robot was to move in a circle, how much faster would the outside wheels have to rotate than the inside wheels? Could you program robots to travel side by side on adjacent circular paths? Open-ended problems such as these can lead to the teacher working alongside the pupils and both parties learning together. The robots themselves provide the feedback as they perform the instructions given to them, whilst learners often use mathematical thinking skills such as trial and improvement as they search for a working solution. Mathematical understanding develops alongside the technological product as learners strive to develop what their robots can do.

Garry has used these activities in regular classes, with pupils working in small groups, and also in an extra-curricular 'robot club'. In both situations, the robots serve not just as an aid to thinking, but also as a substantial motivational tool in the mathematics classroom.

Practical concerns and issues

Hopefully the discussions and examples above have convinced you of some of the cognitive and motivational benefits that can arise from incorporating practical aspects of technology into the mathematics classroom. Before concluding, it is important to recognise some of the issues and limitations that might affect your practice.

First, there are practical issues to do with the cost of the resources involved. The robot equipment described in the case study is fairly expensive, especially if you are seeking to use a whole class set, and initiatives such as this one will most likely need to develop over time, or be supported by grants or additional funding. Not all equipment is as expensive – for instance, the balance beam tool can be constructed relatively cheaply – but cost is generally a relevant factor. You might like to consider talking to the technology department to see what equipment they already possess, or working together with other schools in order to purchase and share more expensive resources.

Second, there are issues of planning and classroom management. Whilst open-ended cross-curricular lessons can be freeing and promote authentic learning, some pupils might not respond entirely positively to changes in structure and provision. In the case of technology, it is worth considering explicitly how equipment will be distributed, managed and returned at the end of the lesson. There may also be additional safety concerns which need to be addressed.

In addition, it is vitally important constantly to challenge the worth of the activities that the pupils are doing. If pupils are going to need three lessons out of a four lesson project to learn how a particular piece of software or apparatus works, and do not do any mathematics until the fourth lesson, it may not be a sensible use of curriculum time, unless they will then go on to use the software in other projects and activities.

The theory of constructionism strongly supports the provision of cross-curricular activities, and offers much to the practising mathematics teacher. However, it can be criticised as possessing an idealised view of learning and schooling, and the learner-centred ideals of constructionism can lead to alternative models of schooling that integrate wider issues of school reform (for example, see Stager (2002)). The challenge of balancing practical limitations, curriculum demands and theoretical ideals is a key one for the cross-curricular practitioner, and your perspective on this balance will undoubtedly develop throughout your career.

Summary

As a subject, technology has a lot to offer the mathematics classroom. It gives rise to a number of contexts that can both demonstrate the purpose of learning a particular mathematical technique or skill and motivate pupils. Many such contexts can, in turn, give rise to activities that involve the use of physical equipment which can motivate pupils further, and possibly improve pupils' internal understanding through external experimentation and play.

Science, technology, engineering and mathematics are often grouped together and referred to as the STEM subjects. This grouping is meaningful, and is often found at the heart of important contemporary topics, such as how to combat global warming, the development of renewable energy sources, the design of better forms of transport and the treatment of diseases. From the mobile phones in the pupils' hands to the exploration of outer space, current STEM research offers teachers a plentiful source of cross-curricular contexts. At the time of writing, the government is funding a number of initiatives to inspire learners in these disciplines, and many of the resources and activities advocate cross-curricular approaches to solving problems. Details of this STEM agenda can be found online at www.stemforum.org.uk.

However, whilst STEM contexts provide a wealth of cross-curricular opportunities, mathematics teaching and learning can also be enhanced through links with many other subjects. The next chapter in this book considers how mathematics can interact with subjects such as English, citizenship and geography, and asks whether mathematical thinking is essential for pupils to develop as critical citizens in today's world.

Professional Standards for QTS

This chapter will help you meet the following Q standards: Q6, Q8, Q10, Q14.

Professional Standards for Teachers

This chapter will help you meet the following core standards: C6, C8, C10, C15.

5

Critical thought and reasoning: mathematics and English, citizenship and geography

Although teachers and textbooks often recognise the close relationship that exists between mathematics and the science and technology subjects, it is frequently implied that mathematics has little to no association with subjects such as English. In one sense this is true; it is clear that there is significantly less content that appears in both subjects' curricula. However, in a deeper sense this understanding is flawed, as the tools learnt in each subject can be used to profoundly benefit the other.

A survey of the modern world shows that numeracy and literacy are profoundly interconnected. Numbers, statistics and probabilistic reasoning permeate most forms of non-fiction writing to the extent that an individual who is literate but not numerate will fail to grasp much of what is reported on the television or in the newspapers. Conversely, a person who is numerate but not literate will have trouble understanding these numbers in their proper context, and they will end up misled, mistaken and misinformed just as often as their innumerate colleague. More immediately, the skills of literacy are also critical in the mathematics classroom whenever a pupil is working with the precise terminology of mathematics, or trying to order and communicate their thoughts on paper.

This chapter begins by considering some of the content links that exist between mathematics and English, and explores the wider roles that literacy and oracy play in the mathematics classroom. It will then move on to argue that a cross-curricular approach to teaching and learning mathematics should extend to the teaching of skills as well as content, and show how this principle is particularly relevant in the cases of English and citizenship.

Finally this chapter will demonstrate how the subject of geography has the potential for both styles of cross-curricular activity examined so far: *physical geography* features a number of contexts which draw on mathematics in a similar manner to science and technology, whilst *human geography* involves scenarios that require critical numerical and statistical reasoning in a similar manner to English and citizenship. In this way, cross-curricular activity in all three of these subjects has the potential to move beyond STEM-based contexts and demonstrate to pupils that mathematical thinking is demanded if they are to develop as critical citizens in the modern world.

Key objectives

By the end of this chapter, you will have:

- Investigated some of the links between the subjects of mathematics, English, citizenship and geography

- Considered the importance of both numeracy and literacy, and appreciated how literacy and oracy are important skills in the mathematics classroom

- Explored how pupils' conceptions of number, statistics and probability are important elements of their development as critical citizens

- Critiqued some activities that bring social and ethical questions into the classroom, and reflected on how you might address similar issues in your own practice

Links between mathematics and English

Although they might not be as numerous as the connections between mathematics and science, there are some content links between the ideas that pupils encounter in mathematics and those that they encounter in English. Some of these links are rather quirky; for instance, pupils might be amused to know that 'simultaneous' and 'equations' are words that contain all five vowels in the English language. The idea of a palindrome, a word that reads the same forwards and backwards, also crosses between the two subjects, as numbers such as 1234321 are also called palindromes. This can lead to some diverting recreational mathematics: how many palindromic numbers are there that are less than 1,000? The square of 212 is 44944; are there any other palindromes that are still palindromes when they are squared? Can you find any tetradic numbers – that is, numbers that are the same when reversed, flipped upside down, or both? Are there any tetradic words?

Mathematics can also be applied in statistical language analysis. In English lessons, pupils are required to recognise some of the different strategies that writers use when constructing a piece of writing. Many of these features can be explored quantitatively. For example, if a pupil was asked to compare how a tabloid and a broadsheet newspaper had reported the same story, they would probably start by looking at the style of writing, the nature of the vocabulary used and the position given to facts in each report. This analysis could then be enhanced by looking at the numbers of letters in the words used, and constructing a comparative bar chart. Relevant summary measures could include the median word length, the number of words used with more than seven letters, the mean number of words in a sentence and the ratio of space afforded to pictures and text in each newspaper.

A more sophisticated measure of language can be found built into many word processing packages. The Flesch Reading Ease test analyses a document and returns a numerical score, typically between 0 and 100; higher values of the score suggest that the document is easier to read. However, it makes no comment on the meaningfulness of the passage. To calculate the Flesch Reading Ease Score, count the total number of sentences, words and syllables in a piece of writing and then substitute them into the following expression:

$$206.835 - 1.015\left(\frac{words}{sentences}\right) - 84.6\left(\frac{syllables}{words}\right)$$

For example, the last paragraph gets a score of approximately 43; if the semi-colon after the '100' was replaced with a full stop this would increase to almost 48. A number of questions which potentially involve ideas and understanding from both English and mathematics can follow from this formula:

- Construct two meaningful sentences, one of which has a very low readability score, and one which has a very high readability score. Comment on what you have written.

- Is there a lowest possible score on this test? Is there a highest possible score on this test? Justify your answer.

- Either research or calculate for yourself a typical value of the Flesch Reading Ease Score for writing from different newspapers or magazines. How might your results be explained by considering the subject matter and/or the target audience?

- An organisation decides that all of its documents must be written so that they have a Reading Ease Score of 50 or higher. Do you think this is a good idea? Why?

- The Gunning Fog index is an alternative score for readability which gives a higher score for 'complex words', which are defined as words of three or more syllables (with some technical exceptions). Do you think this is a fair definition of a 'complex word'?

Quantitative analysis can also be used on foreign languages. More advanced statistical analyses of language have been used to model the links between languages, and suggest ways in which languages have developed and influenced each other over time.

Whilst ideas such as these can give rise to entertaining diversions or investigations that involve ideas from both mathematics and English, it is also important to include activities that develop the wider use of language and literacy in the classroom.

Literacy in mathematics

The prevalence of numbers and other symbols in mathematics can sometimes overshadow the value of encouraging both subject-specific and general literacy skills in mathematics. Yet if pupils are to communicate mathematics effectively, they will need to be able to express themselves in written English, as well as the language of mathematics (Lee and Lawson 1996). Indeed, the very act of writing can itself develop pupils' mathematical learning by getting them to actively reflect on structure and definition and order their thoughts; there is a growing body of research evidence that supports this idea of 'writing to learn'. Unfortunately, analyses of the place of writing in the mathematics classroom repeatedly demonstrate that writing in the mathematics classroom is often restricted to copying or transcribing, and there is no opportunity for pupils to engage in writing as a creative activity (Morgan 1998).

Whilst the task of developing pupils as writers and speakers can seem daunting to the mathematics teacher, it is manageable and can be integrated into regular lessons in a straightforward way. As a starting point, it is usually appropriate to require that pupils use full sentences and proper grammar and spelling when writing up investigations or statistical reports. It can sometimes be constructive to show pupils examples of research-level mathematics to justify this requirement. This can demonstrate to them how professional mathematicians combine symbolic notation with linking sentences and extended sections of exposition and commentary. Another approach is to occasionally set pupils an 'essay' task for their mathematics homework; this type of challenge can develop pupils' understanding of a topic in a way that complements classroom activities. Titles can be largely descriptive, for example, 'Write one hundred words on some mathematics you have seen on the way home from school' or reflective: 'Do you think there is a largest number? Why?'

Subject-specific literacy can be developed in a number of ways in the mathematics classroom. For instance, when ideas and concepts are introduced it can be valuable to explore the origin and meaning of any new words with pupils. It is not sensible to assume that pupils will make links between mathematical terms (for example, 'line' and 'linear equation') or to terms used elsewhere ('cumulative frequency' with 'accumulate'; 'reciprocal' with 'reciprocate'). Explicitly identifying prefixes can help pupils attach meaning to words such as '*circum*ference', '*semi*circle' or '*inter*quartile range'. In some cases, pupils might even meet words such as 'adjacent' in mathematics for the first time, and end up expanding their general vocabulary! Another practical idea is to get pupils who are struggling with their literacy to make a 'maths bookmark' for each new topic on which they note down the spelling of any new words. They can then keep this in their book for reference until the start of the next unit.

Games can also be used to promote the development of mathematical vocabulary. For instance, you might ask the pupils to try and make a verbal chain of mathematical words that stretches around the whole class, wherein each word starts with the last letter of the previous word (length-hypotenuse-equilateral-logic…) and no repeats are allowed. Whilst this is not strictly a cross-curricular activity, it does promote a sensibility that words are a valid part of the mathematical experience. Finally, you might like to introduce poetry into the mathematics classroom. There are a number of published "pi poems" which use words with lengths that correspond to the digits of the mathematical constant pi. Eastaway and Wyndham (2005: 9) phrase this as a challenge: 'Can I find a trick recalling pi easily?' (3.1415926) Another idea is to challenge the pupils to write a poem of a particular form that describes a mathematical idea or concept; for instance, could they write a limerick that described the properties of a kite? Another form of poetry that can be adapted for this exercise is the haiku (Ward-Penny *et al.* 2010). For instance, the following haiku attempts to encapsulate the idea of an asymptote:

Curve comes in to kiss
But still the line forever
Says 'not yet, not yet'

Oracy in the mathematics classroom

The processes of reflecting, ordering and communicating are also important when pupils engage in oral communication and take part in dialogue; the skills of talk that are explicitly addressed in English lessons are in fact central to an empowering pedagogy in mathematics (Alexander 2008; Lampbert and Blunk 1998). It can be difficult to encourage the development of oracy in a subject which has traditionally been associated with one word answers; however, it is crucial as pupils need the space to produce extended verbal responses if they are to gain a sense of ownership over the mathematics. It is often through the pupils verbally expressing ideas themselves that they come to be able to use, conjure and control mathematical ideas (Lee 2006).

To facilitate this, you might like to provide optional frameworks with which pupils can structure their oral responses. For example, self- and peer-assessment of tasks can be organised using a 'what went well' and 'even better if' type structure, where pupils offer two summary sentences that summarise their opinions. It can be profitable speaking to colleagues in the English department and borrowing existing pedagogic structures so that pupils see oral contributions in mathematics as something familiar and less threatening. Drama can also offer scope for pupils' development in this field, and this is discussed further in Chapter 8.

As with any set of activities, not all of these ideas will be suitable for all learners, and it is important to recognise that the pupils in your classes will have a range of facilities with language. Nevertheless, they should all be encouraged to develop these facilities, and it is important that pupils are not overpowered by 'teacher talk' as the prime mode of communication. Both pupil literacy and oracy have critical roles to play in the mathematics classroom, and well thought out uses of language can stimulate learning and guide pupils towards instances of higher-order mathematical thinking.

Shared processes in English, mathematics and citizenship

Many of the ideas presented in this book so far have been centred on content- or context-based opportunities for cross-curricular learning which draw specific ideas or situations from other subjects to illustrate and motivate pupils' study of mathematics. However, it is important to recognise that a thorough cross-curricular approach to teaching and learning mathematics involves an explicit consideration of shared skills as well as a connected presentation of knowledge.

The shift in focus from content to skills can be simultaneously profound and subtle. For instance, when a pupil is learning to classify quadrilaterals in mathematics, they are not only learning about quadrilaterals but also developing their facility with the skill of classifying. This same skill is used in biology to classify organisms, and in technology to classify resistant materials according to their properties. The new version of the secondary National Curriculum is structured in such a way that it is sometimes possible, and indeed advantageous, to teach some skills in tandem with other subjects, and hence add an extra dimension of cross-curricular activity.

A comparison of the skills listed in the programmes of study suggests that this is very true in the case of mathematics and English. The National Curriculum for English (QCA 2007: 60–99) holds that the following skills are 'key processes' in Key Stage 3 English:

- Present information and points of view clearly and appropriately in different contexts… including the more formal
- Extract and interpret information, events, main points and ideas from texts
- Use formal and impersonal language and concise expression
- Develop logical arguments and cite evidence

A strong case can be made that quantitative reasoning plays a part in each of these statements. Pupils cannot be expected to develop fully rounded skills of comprehension in the modern world, or to be able to persuasively communicate a complex factual argument without using numbers or statistics. From a cross-curricular point of view, this means that the English teacher has a responsibility to include quantitative elements in some of the texts that they present, and to encourage the proper use of these aspects.

On the other hand, the National Curriculum for mathematics (QCA 2007: 138–163) identifies the following as 'key processes' in Key Stage 3 mathematics:

- Form convincing arguments based on findings and make general statements
- Engage with someone else's mathematical reasoning in the context of a problem or particular situation
- Communicate findings effectively
- Engage in mathematical discussion of results

These processes resonate strongly with the aims of the English curriculum listed above. A parallel case can therefore be made that the skills of comprehension, communication and argument taught in English also have a place in the mathematics classroom. The mathematics teacher could benefit from embracing many of the methods used in English teaching in order to improve their pupils' understanding of the relevance and importance of mathematics, as well as their pupils' communication skills and use of argument.

A further cross-curricular link can be made with citizenship. Critical thinking and enquiry forms a key part of the citizenship curriculum (QCA 2007: 26–49) which provides a third set of related 'key processes':

- Research, plan, and undertake enquiries into issues and problems using a range of information and sources
- Communicate an argument, taking account of different viewpoints and drawing on what they have learnt through research, action and debate
- Justify their argument, giving reasons to try to persuade others to think again, change or support them

Again, there is a definite relationship between the processes contained in this list and those detailed above. In this way there is significant potential for all three subjects to work together in order to help develop pupils' critical apparatus, and through this to encourage pupils to appreciate the function and importance of mathematics.

As an example of this potential, the next part of this chapter looks at the facilities of numerical and statistical reasoning, which are important elements of a pupil's mathematical facility, and considers how these capacities can be developed in mathematics lessons through the use of situations, sensibilities, skills and understandings drawn from English and citizenship.

Understanding number in real-life contexts

What percentage of the UK population would identify themselves as ethnically 'white'? How much money does the British government spend on secondary education each year? How many of the ten warmest years in England on record have occurred since

1990? It is unlikely that you know the exact figures – and the chances are that at least one of your answers will be significantly different from the correct value. (For completeness, the answers are 92 per cent (according to the 2001 census), £88 billion (according to the 2009 budget) and all ten (according to the Office for National Statistics).

If you were far off the mark, you are in good company. Blastland and Dilnot (2008) administered a multiple choice survey to a number of senior civil servants. The answers they gave about topics such as the economy, tax and means-tested benefits were wildly incorrect. It would appear that accuracy does not necessarily improve with responsibility.

It is an unfortunate truth that, in terms of data at least, people are often comfortable arguing from a position of ignorance. Luckily, even the most convincing piece of empty rhetoric can be deflated with the power of well-researched data. Although numbers and percentages might not make for the most gripping speech, they offer a strong foundation to an argument, and an excellent weapon against faulty reasoning. This is a valuable lesson for pupils to learn, so if they are making a case for human rights, it is important to get them to find out how many prisoners of conscience there are in the world today; and if they are arguing for better recycling facilities, it is important they research the capacity and usage of current resources.

Whilst pupils are most likely to carry out such research outside of the mathematics classroom, many of the numbers involved will undoubtedly be very large, and it is the responsibility of the mathematics teacher to equip each pupil with tools for dealing with them. For instance, one way of addressing the 'number numbness' described in Chapter 2 is to encourage pupils to visualise numbers such as one million and one billion. One strategy for doing this is to recognise that one million is $100 \times 100 \times 100$, or 100 cubed. Therefore, if you used sugar cubes to build a large cube which had a side length of 100 sugar cubes, the resulting structure would be made out of one million sugar cubes. Alternatively, you might ask pupils to estimate how many grains of sand could fit into a pint glass, or how long it would take for an 'average' person to earn one million pounds. These sorts of activities can make good starters.

Another popular visualisation exercise is to re-imagine the world as a village of 100 people. If all the demographic ratios were held constant, how many people would be male, and how many female? How many would be white? How many would live in Africa? How many would be heterosexual? Rather than just telling the pupils the answers, it would be good practice for them to do the calculations themselves. Some of the figures quoted are very challenging, and lead into important citizenship issues – for example, it has been said that 67 would be illiterate, 50 would be malnourished, and only one would have any form of higher education.

A further challenge is to ask pupils to break down a large number that has been reported in the news or elsewhere, and ask what it actually *means*. For instance, Boyle and Roddick (2004: 29) report that the National Health Service buys 55,000 gallons of orange juice each year. This seems like a very large number, but what does it *mean*? How many cups of orange juice would a gallon produce? How many patients does the NHS have staying in hospital each year? On average, how many meals would they require during their stay? Is this still a very large number?

These kinds of activities practice skills such as estimation and ratio whilst developing pupils' mathematical literacy and also encourage them to go on and use quantitative elements in other subjects such as English and citizenship. Using a 'real-life' figure as the basis for a starter or plenary exercise can also serve to motivate pupils and demonstrate to them the value of what they have just been studying.

Practical task

Boyle and Roddick (2004) have published a book full of statistics which are designed to make the reader laugh, gasp and think in equal measure. They encourage the reader to ask whether 'they are just general numbers about people that are meaningless when it comes to applying them to individuals' (p. 5).

The following three numbers have been taken from their book. Try to 'unpack' each number for yourself, noting down what mathematical skills you practice in the process, and determining what the number might mean, if it means anything at all.

- The toilet rolls used every year in Japan would circle the equator ten times.
- The typical American teenager sees 360,000 adverts before they graduate.
- Seven million mobile phones are destroyed every year by being dropped into water.

Developing powers of statistical argument

Whilst numbers in real-life reports are confusing for people, statistics are a veritable minefield. Huff (1954: 10) summarises the situation succinctly: 'the secret language of statistics, so appealing in a fact-minded culture, is employed to sensationalize, inflate, confuse and oversimplify.' It is part of the mathematics teachers' remit to equip pupils with the critical tools they require to both use statistics themselves, and to talk back to the statistics of others.

One way of getting pupils to structure their own use of statistics is to borrow a pedagogical technique from English. English teachers often use the framework of 'point-evidence-explanation' to support their pupils in writing essays. This involves the pupil making a statement, then selecting one or two relevant quotations to justify their point. Finally they explain what the quotations mean and why they are relevant, and then link their point to the overall argument. A similar model could be used to encourage pupils to use summary statistics and graphical representations in a balanced way. For instance, pupils could start by saying that there is a difference in the heights of boys and girls in their class (point), demonstrate this with two histograms (evidence), then point out the key features of the histograms that they feel show the salient differences (explanation). A possible additional benefit of this approach is that pupils might begin to appreciate that statistics, like the evidence they gather in English, are bound up with meaning and purpose, and are different in character from mathematical 'facts' such as $3 + 7 = 10$.

Pupils also benefit from a cross-curricular approach when they are learning how to question statistics. The abstract statement that 'correlation does not imply causation' can sound rather hollow to a pupil who is encountering the idea for the first time. However, the logical relationship becomes more meaningful as it is illustrated with examples. These examples can often be drawn from the headlines: for instance, in 1999 a study found that young children who sleep with a light left on in the room are more likely to develop myopia later in life, and many parents concluded that leaving a light on could damage their children's health. However, later research found that there was a common causative factor; parents who had myopia were more likely to leave a light on, and also more likely to have children with myopia. There are many other such examples which serve well as cautionary tales.

Another important idea that is best introduced through examples is 'regression towards the mean'. Simply put, this principle states that many quantities contain natural variation, and if the first measurement is very high or low, the next measurement will tend to be closer to the centre of the distribution. Whilst this might seem like common sense when stated abstractly, regression fallacies often come up in real-life arguments. Speed cameras are often placed at locations where there have been a very high number of accidents; any decrease in the accident rate is then attributed to the presence of the camera. Intervention strategies are often applied in schools where the pass rate is very low; any improvement in the results is then attributed to the intervention strategies. This is not to say that speed cameras and intervention strategies do not have positive effects; only that we must be aware of 'post hoc, ergo propter hoc' reasoning. If pupils can grasp this form of counter-argument, they most certainly have a tool to 'persuade others to think again' in citizenship, and at the same time they have developed their understanding of the mathematical concept of a distribution.

Before moving on, it is worth noting that human judgement and argument can be distorted by cognitive illusions (Pohl 2004). For example, people often reason falsely with probability. Directly confronting examples of this flawed reasoning in mathematics lessons can help pupils to develop a more precise understanding of probability as a concept whilst also equipping them for their wider learning. One of the most common errors is known as the conjunction fallacy. The psychologists Tversky and Kahneman (1982: 91–96) demonstrated this fallacy by giving people the following description:

> Linda is 31 years old, single, outspoken, and very bright. She majored in philosophy. As a student, she was deeply concerned with issues of discrimination and social justice, and also participated in anti-nuclear demonstrations.

They then asked their participants to rank eight statements in order of likelihood. These statements included 'Linda is a bank teller' (option A) and 'Linda is a bank teller who is active in the feminist movement' (option B). Eighty-five per cent of the people tested ranked option B as being more probable than option A. However, this is illogical, for if B is true, A also has to be true. Therefore the probability of A has to be equal to, or greater than that of B. Although this might appear inconsequential, it is plausible that this kind of flawed reasoning, based on a 'representative heuristic' can be a factor in more significant social and political arguments.

Ethical values and mathematics

Mathematics, then, is a tool which can help equip pupils to become critical citizens; the National Curriculum holds that 'the emphasis on analysing and justifying conclusions in mathematical situations helps prepare pupils for taking critical and analytical approaches to real-life situations' (QCA 2007, 'Mathematics and the National Curriculum aims' section). It is fair to say that this preparation can only be enhanced by placing real-life situations alongside mathematical activity in the classroom.

Before moving on, though, it is important to recognise that these situations often bring with them difficult questions of ethics and values. It might seem odd thinking of mathematics in these terms; as a subject, mathematics is often portrayed as objective, neutral and value-free. However, outside of the classroom the use and application of mathematics is frequently value-laden, and often political. Surely this should be reflected in the classroom? On the other hand, it might be argued that some topics should not be discussed in the mathematics classroom. Perhaps some issues should be kept separate to ensure that they are treated with the respect they deserve and not used as a vehicle for other learning.

The National Curriculum talks about *all* subjects contributing to the moral development of pupils; it can also be argued that since mathematics is so important in our modern society, it would in fact be improper to attempt to teach it in a moral vacuum. MacKernan (2000: 45) argues that 'a discipline that draws a veil over inequality, injustice and human suffering, when it could illuminate it, is not beautiful, but ugly.' Ultimately it is up to each individual practitioner to find and justify a balanced approach to dealing with sensitive issues in the classroom.

Reflective task

Although it is an important part of the mathematics teacher's job to link their subject to the real world, each teacher has to manage this task in a way that they are personally comfortable with.

Each of the following issues could theoretically be used as a citizenship context in a mathematics classroom. Which of these would you personally be happy to use? Which do you think you would avoid?

- Credit card debt and UK spending
- Distribution of ASBOs in the local area by postcode
- Sustainable resources and global warming
- Death statistics from current or recent wars
- The spread of sexually transmitted diseases
- Different systems of voting and election

The discussion above has hopefully convinced you that a cross-curricular approach to teaching mathematics stretches beyond the use of contexts and knowledge drawn from other subjects, and includes a sensitivity to teaching skills in such a way that they are readily available for pupils to use in other subjects. Ideally this should lead to a reflexive state of affairs; the pupil's appreciation and understanding of mathematics enhances, and is in turn enhanced by, their use of mathematics in other subjects.

This principle applies to all subject areas, not just English and citizenship. It is valuable to interrogate the curriculum of each subject not only to find out what content is shared, but also to identify common skills and processes. This dual approach to cross-curricular activity is particularly evident in the field of geography.

Mathematics and geography

Like 'technology', 'geography' is a term with a very wide range of application. Traditionally geography has been separated into two fields: physical geography and human geography. However, both of these are themselves incredibly broad in scope, and in this way they give rise to a number of contexts which can be used for illustrative purposes in the mathematics classroom.

Physical geography can be understood as a collection of scientific disciplines which each study a particular aspect of the Earth and its environment. It includes fields as diverse as climatology (the study of the climate), glaciology (the study of glaciers and ice sheets), oceanography (the study of the oceans and seas) and pedology (the study of soils). These disciplines often give rise to specific physical relationships which can be modelled mathematically and used as illustrations in mathematics lessons.

Conversely, human geography is more akin to a social science, and is concerned with patterns of human activity. In this way it encompasses the study of standards of living, health and disease, politics and tourism. As human geography is more focused on the study of abstract patterns and trends rather than physical systems, it tends to give rise to areas of study which can be explored and understood using statistical methods.

This distinction is not absolute, and many geographers move between these two branches; however, it does serve to illustrate how a cross-curricular approach to geography involves an appreciation of both content and skills.

Physical geography contexts for mathematics

Physical geography contains a number of familiar ideas which can be used in the mathematics classroom. For instance, the idea of time zones around the globe can serve as a useful illustration of negative numbers. However, the diversity that exists within the many branches of physical geography also gives rise to a multitude of more unusual contexts. Three areas of study are offered here as examples:

Glaciology

The study of glaciers is of particular interest at the time of writing, as receding glaciers are held to be a consequence of global warming. To investigate such claims, pupils would have to gather and interpret data that involves significant seasonal variation; glaciologists have to interpret such information to estimate accumulation and ablation rates for glaciers and make predictions. The growth (or shrinkage) of a glacier can also be modelled using the following formula:

$$B_n = P - R - E$$

where B_n is the net balance of the glacier, P is the precipitation over the glacier basin, R is the total run off as measured by stream gauges, and E is the amount of water lost through evaporation. Of course, many of these measures are not exact, so a formula like this provides a good opportunity to consider and discuss the combined effect of measurement errors.

Marine pollution

Another area of study with environmental aspects is marine pollution. Pupils are likely to have seen some of the dramatic images that emerge when oil slicks reach the shore and affect local wildlife, and they might be interested to know that mathematics is used to model the spread of oil slicks at sea. Whilst the full models use differential equations and the idea of diffusion, it is possible to set up some basic scenarios for use in the secondary classroom; for instance, given that an oil slick travels downwind at approximately 4 per cent of the wind speed, use a scale map to estimate the time of day that the oil will reach different parts of the shoreline. The study of marine pollution also uses a number of mathematical tools introduced at secondary school level; for instance, the relative effect of different polluting agents is determined using a cumulative frequency method where the 'median lethal concentration' is the concentration that will kill half of a population after a set period of time.

Natural catastrophes

Natural catastrophes provide a rich source of mathematical contexts that can be explored in the secondary classroom. For instance, consider earthquakes: the Richter scale that is used to measure the intensity of earthquakes is logarithmic; the idea of epicentre location and intensity isoseismals can develop the concept of loci; and pupils might investigate whether there is a correlation between the number of casualties in an earthquake and its intensity, and try to explain their findings using their understanding of human geography. Pupils might also use conditional probabilities to measure the relative effectiveness of earthquake and tornado warning systems. Various formulae exist to map the features of hurricanes, tornadoes and tsunamis, and even extraterrestrial impacts can be described using mathematics; the diameter of a formed crater, D, grows in proportion to the cube root of the kinetic energy, K, of the asteroid: $D \propto K^{1/3}$. Finally, it is also interesting to note that some recent research suggests that landslides might have a self-similar aspect, and that fractal geometry could help us understand and predict future landslides.

Mathematics as a tool in human geography

In contrast to physical geography, human geography is more concerned with the intangible aspects of how humans interact with their environment and with each other. This does not rule out the use of quantitative techniques, but it tends to gives rise to situations where mathematics is used to interpret situations rather than describe them.

Tourism geography

For instance, one issue raised in tourism geography is the effect that tourism has on natural resources such as a region's water supply. This is a particular concern in drier regions where water scarcity is already an issue that can be exacerbated by increasing numbers of tourists. Mathematics offers pupils a set of skills with which to collect, interpret and present data on how the level of tourism, the level of water consumption and the volume of waste water produced have all changed over time. Similar methods could be used to try and quantify the environmental impact of specific features, such as a golf course.

Development geography

Development geography is concerned with the study of the standard of living in different regions or countries of the world. This discipline relies extensively on statistics; many quantitative indicators are used in development geography, including birth and death rates, the adult literacy rate and the gross domestic product (GDP). In 1990 the United Nations proposed a composite measure for the quality of life, known as the Human Development Index, or HDI. This is a scaled measure that gives a value between 0 and 1 for each country, where 1 represents a very high standard of living (in 2009 the United Kingdom achieved a score of 0.947). The exact formula is not included here for reasons of space, but it is a uniformly weighted combination of the Life Expectancy Index, the United Nations' Education Index and the country's GDP, expressed as an index. This gives rise to a number of interesting questions: why were these three measures chosen? Should any others be included? Should all of the factor indices used be equally weighted? What happens if we change the construction of this index? Do most countries attain a HDI score similar to what you would expect?

Population geography and demography

These involve the study of human populations, both spatially and statistically. Locally, pupils can attempt to use the concepts of area and density to examine whether a settlement is nuclear, linear, or dispersed. More globally, pupils can use statistics to explore patterns of migration, employment and mortality. Many websites exist that provide up-to-date raw data for pupils to use and representations of population development; these include www.gapminder.org and www.breathingearth.net.

One statistical tool that is often used in geography to represent spatial patterns and distributions is the choropleth map. These maps, where areas are coloured or shaded to show the value of the quantity being measured, are readily available in the front of atlases, and you might like to consider borrowing some atlases from the geography department and using them in the mathematics classroom. Choropleth maps are also used to represent demographic patterns that have relevance in other subject areas, such as RE; for instance, Figure 5.1 is based on 2001 census data, and shows the Muslim population as a proportion of the population in different areas of England.

Before concluding, it is valuable to note that many of the contexts discussed involve significant elements from more than two subjects. Mathematical contexts drawn from physical geography typically include elements of overlap with science, and examples taken from human geography are often connected to issues and topics that are likely to be discussed in citizenship lessons. Some activities, such as calculating your own ecological footprint, involve ideas from all of these subjects. Here, as with many of the other examples outlined in this chapter, it is impossible to demarcate exactly where one subject ends and another begins. Whilst this can be problematic in a practical school sense, it is a natural consequence of starting with authentic activities, and is arguably an inevitable part of cross-curricular activity.

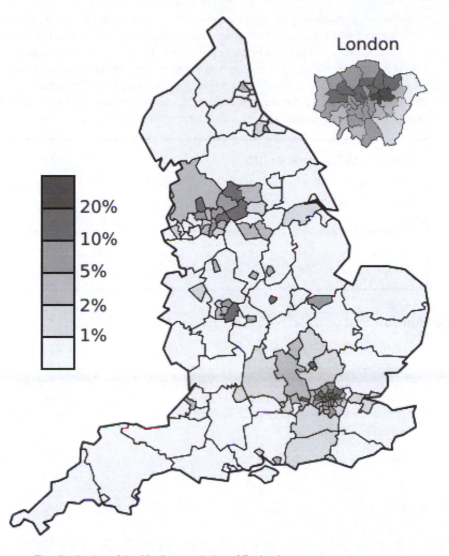

Figure 5.1 The distribution of the Muslim population of England.

Summary

The definition offered at the start of Chapter 1 proposed that 'a cross-curricular approach to teaching is characterised by sensitivity towards, and a synthesis of, knowledge, skills and understandings from various subject areas.' (Savage 2011: 8–9) As we move from considering the STEM subjects to the wider curriculum, we have to be aware of each of the aspects contained in this statement; whilst geography-based contexts might involve additional knowledge, a cross-curricular integration of English might instead entail sensitivity to the skills of argument and writing, and the use of ideas from citizenship is likely to require awareness of how to deal with controversial and emotive issues.

Such a nuanced approach to cross-curricular activity in mathematics is more challenging for the teacher than simply importing contexts from other subjects, and it raises a number of additional pedagogical issues. However, whilst teaching in this way might be more challenging, it is also more interesting and quite possibly more effective; it can open the door to a wealth of opportunities that can stimulate debate and engage the pupils in new and exciting ways. It is also ultimately essential if pupils are to develop an appreciation of mathematics as an authentic tool for critical citizenship.

Professional Standards for QTS

This chapter will help you meet the following Q standards: Q6, Q8, Q10, Q14, Q15, Q17, Q18, Q19, Q23.

Professional Standards for Teachers

This chapter will help you meet the following core standards: C6, C8, C10, C15, C16, C17, C18, C19, C27.

Further reading

Morgan, C. (2001) 'The place of pupil writing in learning, teaching and assessing mathematics', in Gates, P. (ed.), *Issues in Mathematics Teaching*, (pp. 232–244).

This considers some of the issues raised in this chapter in more detail, asking why mathematics teachers should bother about writing. It argues that mathematical writing activities can not only improve mathematical thinking, but also pupils' attitudes towards mathematics.

6

Different perspectives: mathematics and history, RE and art

One of the great benefits of cross-curricular activity is that it can encourage pupils to consider each of the included subjects in a new light. This is particularly true in the case of mathematics, and previous chapters have already illustrated how cross-curricular activities can help pupils appreciate the power and relevance of mathematics in the modern world.

Cross-curricular activities also offer opportunities for pupils to question and develop their view of the essential nature of mathematics. Many people have come to see mathematics as an absolute, unchanging set of facts and methods, and perhaps unsurprisingly this narrow and impersonal view has been thought to lead to disaffection amongst pupils. However, by connecting mathematics with subjects such as history, RE and art it is possible to demonstrate that mathematics is not only cross-curricular, but also cross-cultural. Encouraging pupils to recognise that mathematics is a socially and culturally situated practice that has developed over time can, in turn, help them develop their own identity as emerging mathematicians.

This chapter will introduce a number of activities and approaches which can be used to explore mathematics in this way, as well as discussing some of the central issues that surround the presentation of mathematics as a fundamentally human endeavour.

Key objectives

By the end of this chapter, you will have:

- Investigated some of the links between the subjects of mathematics, history, RE and art
- Considered the potential benefits of teaching topics drawn from the history of mathematics
- Reflected on the idea of mathematics as a cross-cultural practice, and seen how this might be represented in the classroom
- Recognised some of the ways in which mathematical ideas are integrated into religious practice
- Appreciated the relationship between geometry and art

Mathematics and history

The most immediate link between history and mathematics is perhaps the use of dates. At the most basic level this can lead to simple arithmetical calculations, but it is important to have some appreciation of the calendar system: for example, although Queen Victoria lived from 1819 to 1901, she died at the age of 81, not 82, and there is still debate over exactly when the millennium started! Dates and time travel can also serve as a metaphor with which to introduce directed numbers. For example, if a time traveller is in 2011 and wishes to travel to the beginning of the Second World War in 1939, he must journey backwards 72 years: 2011 + -72 = 1939. Alternatively, the BC/AD system of labelling dates can also be used as an illustration of the positive and negative branches of the number line. (It is important to recognise, however, that the BC/AD scheme does not include a year 0.)

The study of history also requires elements of numerical and statistical reasoning in much the same way as geography did in the previous chapter. For instance, the National Curriculum for history requires that pupils are taught 'the way in which the lives, beliefs, ideas and attitudes of people in Britain have changed over time' (QCA 2007: 166). This type of study can be enhanced by looking at quantitative measures, such as a time series graph that displays the changes in life expectancy over the last five hundred years, or pie charts that demonstrate how the religious profile of Britain has developed over the last century. Census data can be a valuable source of information for investigating historical questions in some detail, and the website www.censusatschool.org.uk contains a number of free resources which locate statistics in a historical context, including a set of data which allows pupils to explore whether children were shorter 150 years ago.

Professional historians also use mathematics in a number of other ways, some of which can be introduced into the classroom. Archaeologists, for example, use methods such as radiocarbon dating to establish the approximate age of finds. These are based around exponential decay, and so they can be introduced explicitly to pupils studying first-order differential equations. Statistical methods such as chi-squared tests are used to help archaeologists test theories about patterns and associations in their finds; for instance, whether certain types of grave goods are linked to the sex of the occupant of that grave (Shennan 1983). Any conclusions reached about archaeological finds also have to consider issues of sampling and bias.

There are many other similar ways to link mathematics with historical contexts. However, whilst contexts such as these are both valid and useful, it is possible to inculcate a much stronger connection between the two subjects by moving to consider how mathematics itself is located within history.

Mathematics through history

Although mathematics has a strong abstract and logical aspect to its nature, it remains a discipline that has been developed and implemented by human beings. Some mathematicians have proposed that this might alter the way in which mathematics can be viewed:

Mathematics does have a subject matter, and its statements are meaningful. The meaning, however, is to be found in the shared understanding of human beings, not in an external nonhuman reality … it deals with human meanings and is intelligible only within the context of culture. In other words, mathematics is a humanistic study. It is one of the humanities.

(Davis and Hersh 1983: 410)

You might not agree fully with this statement, but it is certainly fair to say that mathematics is socially and culturally situated to some extent; the mathematics that was used five hundred years ago in South America was markedly different in both its nature and scope to the mathematics used today in Western Europe. The idea of mathematics as a developing discipline is not always obvious to pupils, especially when teachers have, either implicitly or explicitly, acted in such a way that suggests mathematics is a purely abstract body of knowledge, unchanging and unquestioned. Unfortunately this position can contribute to pupils developing views of mathematics as elitist and impersonal, and these views can in turn lead to disaffection with the subject (Nardi and Steward 2003).

Recognising the historical development of mathematics can help to ameliorate this situation. For example, your pupils might find it interesting to discover that probability was developed in the seventeenth century by Pascal and Fermat in order to better understand games of chance; it can now be used in the secondary classroom in a very similar way. It can also be helpful to acknowledge the sometimes arbitrary nature of mathematical conventions – for instance there is no unarguable reason that when rounding 8.5 to the nearest integer we should always round up to 9. In fact many alternative tie-breaking rules exist that are designed to be less biased, such as rounding to the even number (in this case 8) or randomly choosing between the two integers. Conventions such as this one have been established and reinforced over time.

Once mathematics is seen as a developing field of study, it is natural to introduce contemporary mathematicians and contemporary mathematics into the secondary classroom. This is particularly relevant in the curriculum area of decision mathematics, where most of the algorithms and techniques are relatively new, and many of the key mathematicians are still alive. Another way of making mathematics more contemporary is to challenge pupils to explore problems that are currently unsolved, such as the Goldbach conjecture: that every even integer greater than 2 can be written as the sum of two prime numbers. This has been unproven since 1742; could one of your pupils be the one to see something new in it?

In many cases, pupils can develop a deeper level of understanding by viewing mathematics through the lens of history. As they explore how concepts have developed over time, and in different cultures, pupils often begin to look beyond the individual algorithms and rules to see the underlying structures of the mathematics. This is particularly true in the case of different number systems.

Representations of number through history

Although we often take it for granted today, our system of numbers (the 'Hindu–Arabic numeral system') was not used in the Western world until the Middle Ages. Throughout history, a number of other systems have been, and are still being used to represent and manipulate numbers. Historical systems were often constructed around bases other than 10; for instance, the Aztec system was vigesimal (base 20) and used pictorial symbols that represented 1, 20, 400 and 8,000. This system of notation gives rise to a number of questions for pupils to explore: can all numbers be formed by adding together lots of 1, 20, 400 and 8,000? Which number less than 10,000 would require the most pictures?

The Babylonians tended to use a base 60 system. Details of this are given by Eagle (1995) who also offers some reproductions of marks found on recovered clay tablets. By looking at these reproductions pupils can extract the mathematics from an authentic, original source. Using historical sources in the mathematics classroom can add an extra dimension to cross-curricular practice, as it encourages pupils to employ some of the evidence handling skills they have developed in history, and ask what they can learn from each source. An interesting example of this process concerns the famous Babylonian clay tablet 'Plimpton 322', which consists of three columns of numbers that have been interpreted as a list of Pythagorean triples, over a thousand years prior to Pythagoras himself. The exact purpose of the tablet has been debated extensively; Robson (2002) offers a commentary which attempts to balance a mathematical analysis with a historical one, and suggests that the tablet is in fact a teacher's aid.

Many pupils might already be familiar with basic Roman numerals, as they are still used today on clock faces, in certain sports contexts (such as the first XV of a rugby union club) and even in music theory notation. It is interesting to consider why Roman numerals are no longer widely used today, and what advantages the positional notation of our Hindu-Arabic system offers; is it easy enough to add and subtract Roman numerals? How challenging is it to perform a multiplication, such as XLVII multiplied by XI, compared with 47 x 11? The Roman system also had no specific symbol for zero.

Another interesting development of the use of number came with the Ancient Egyptians. Although their system of notation developed over time, Egyptian fractions tended to be written as the sum of unit fractions, that is, fractions where the numerator is equal to 1. For instance, $\frac{11}{24}$ would be written (using hieroglyphs) as $\frac{1}{3} + \frac{1}{8}$. Again, this gives rise to a number of valuable questions for the mathematics classroom: can all fractions be written in this form? Is there more than one way of writing some fractions in an 'Egyptian' way? Can you devise a method for systematically converting any rational number into a sum of Egyptian fractions?

One set of such fractions has a particular historical and cultural meaning. The 'Eye of Horus' is a key Ancient Egyptian symbol which has been linked to more recent symbols such as the 'evil eye' and the 'all-seeing eye'. However, it also has a strong link to arithmetic. In Egyptian notation the six fractions $\frac{1}{2}$, $\frac{1}{4}$, $\frac{1}{8}$, $\frac{1}{16}$, $\frac{1}{32}$ and $\frac{1}{64}$ were all represented by hieroglyphs which symbolised the senses of the body and thought. These six hieroglyphs combine to form the 'Eye of Horus', which in turn represented the number 1 (see figure 6.1). The detail behind this forms a fantastic narrative which weaves together arithmetic, mythology and symbolism, and scholars have long speculated about the possible meaning that might be implied by the missing $\frac{1}{64}$.

There are many other historical systems of symbols and algorithms that can be used productively in the secondary classroom to help develop pupils' understanding of mathematical concepts; for example, you might go on to consider and compare some of the methods that different cultures have used to calculate square roots.

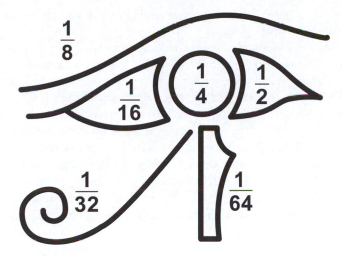

Figure 6.1 The Eye of Horus fractions.

Whilst the examples discussed are undoubtedly interesting, it is important to recognise at this point that many of the historical periods being discussed are not typically covered in the secondary school, and so you may need to provide some historical background before proceeding with the mathematics. Alternatively, you might choose to work more closely in collaboration with colleagues who teach history, and focus on historical contexts which are seen as mutually beneficial.

Mathematics as history

Although mathematics has sometimes been portrayed as a staid and abstract discipline, mathematicians and their work have often featured at key moments in history. This is perhaps unsurprising; after all, mathematics is a discipline which has contributed extensively to the influential fields of finance, business and, via science, weapons design. It can be motivating for some developments in mathematics to be presented in their wider historical context.

One example is the use of weapons developed by Archimedes during the siege of Syracuse (c. 214–212 BC). Whilst many of his weapons have been reproduced from historical accounts and shown to be workable, there is doubt about one particular weapon: the heat ray of Archimedes. This weapon was made up of a large number of reflectors that were placed along the shore in the approximate shape of a parabola, and arranged so as to focus the heat of the sun on a particular ship, causing it to burst into flames. It would be an interesting cross-curricular exercise to examine both the mathematics and the science of this idea, exploring how easy it would be to get wood to reach its flash point, and perhaps performing a live experiment.

A more modern example of mathematics in warfare is the use of the Enigma machine to encrypt messages during the Second World War. The Enigma machine used a combination of rotors to encode messages into ciphers, and this procedure can be represented mathematically in terms of permutations and their inverses. The messages that were deciphered by mathematicians during the war were extremely valuable in helping the war effort.

The history of cryptography is replete with tales that can be brought into the mathematics classroom (Singh 2000). One elementary example is the Caesar cipher. This is a shift substitution cipher, which means that each letter is replaced by a corresponding letter which is a preset distance away in the alphabet. For example, if the distance was set as $+10$, each A would be replaced with K, B would be replaced by L and so on. This cipher, which embodies the basics of modular arithmetic, was said to have been used by Julius Caesar to communicate with his generals. Another method that bears his name is the Caesar square. To decode a message in a Caesar square, such as ASIRSCCCMCRUUAOORLTDSRAHE, write the cipher text in a square array and then read the columns vertically. This method can be made more secure by using different sizes of rectangles rather than just squares. A code phrase at the beginning of a message could tell the reader what size rectangle to use. For instance, "Greetings, friend" could instruct the recipient to rewrite the coded message in a 9 by 6 rectangle.

Outside of warfare, mathematicians have also been influential in the wider development of society. One example is the astronomer Copernicus, who proposed a mathematical model that suggested that the earth moved around the sun, rather than vice versa. Over time this work became one of the starting points of a scientific revolution, as well as affecting the place of the Catholic Church as the head of science as well as religion. On occasion mathematics has been developed by historical figures largely famous for other reasons: the seventeenth century philosopher René Descartes, famous for the statement 'I think, therefore I am' was also a keen mathematician who gave his name to the Cartesian co-ordinate system, and the twentieth president of the United States, James Garfield, produced a novel proof of Pythagoras' theorem in 1876. Florence Nightingale was a keen statistician, and invented the polar area graph to help raise awareness of the casualty figures of the Crimean war (Magnello 2010).

Ultimately, the creation and development of all of mathematics has happened against the background of history (Katz 1998). By recognising this, the cross-curricular teacher of mathematics is no longer limited to using examples of mathematical skills in the academic study of history, but is able to consider the development of mathematics through history, and the role of mathematics in history. Whilst these approaches need to be handled with care (Rogers 2010) they can enhance and motivate the study of mathematics in a number of ways; a further example of this approach is given in the case study in Chapter 9.

Mathematics as a cross-cultural discipline

The explicit teaching of the history of mathematics can also help pupils to explore one of the cross-curriculum dimensions of the National Curriculum: cultural diversity. The examples above have started to illustrate how mathematics is a discipline that is not only cross-curricular, but cross-cultural. It is important to recognise that much of the current teaching of mathematics can be criticised for implicitly presenting the subject in both an androcentric and Eurocentric way (Joseph 1991). Whilst it might be strange to think of mathematics teaching as being in any way sexist or racist, it is surprisingly easy to argue that it contains a definite bias.

Practical task

Consider an English school pupil's experience of learning mathematics at secondary school. Briefly note down the names of any mathematicians that you think they would come across in the classroom, such as Pythagoras, Fibonacci, Newton and Euclid.

Now sketch out three overlapping circles in the style of a Venn diagram. Label one of the circles 'dead', a second circle 'white' and the final circle 'male'. Place the names of the mathematicians in the region of the Venn diagram where they belong. What do you notice? Do all of the regions contain at least one name? How easy do you find it to think of mathematicians who would belong in any empty regions that remain?

There is a definite value, then, in presenting mathematics from different cultures and countering the implicit Eurocentric bias. However, this must be attempted carefully. It is important neither to present cross-cultural activities as 'fun' alternatives that deviate from a European norm, nor to imply that non-European cultures only used basic ideas of number that were quickly superseded by the mathematics of the Ancient Greeks and subsequently relegated to the pages of history.

One way to address this misconception directly is to uncover the history of some well-known mathematics. Pythagoras' theorem, for example, is attributed to the Greek mathematician Pythagoras and dated at approximately 500 BC. However, we have already seen some evidence of so-called Pythagorean triples on the tablet Plimpton 322, dated at around 1800 BC; it appears that Pythagoras may have generalised and represented an existing mathematical result. The ideas of Pythagoras' theorem, as well as some ideas about quadratic equations, also turn up in the ancient Chinese book *Jiuzhang Suanshu*, or *Nine Chapters on the Mathematical Art*, dated at about AD 100 (Eagle 1995: 24–30). Another example of this nature is Pascal's triangle; it is named after the French mathematician Blaise Pascal who developed the arrangement in a publication dated 1653, but the coefficients and their patterns were known to Indian, Persian and Chinese mathematicians many hundreds of years beforehand. Finally, whilst the history of algebra is long and complicated, much of the form and nature of the field was developed by Indian and Islamic mathematicians, and the word 'algebra' itself comes from the Arabic language, 'al-jabr' meaning 'restoration' (Joseph 1991: 324).

Specific examples of mathematics from different cultures can also be used as starting points for mathematical investigation. An examination of different types of Celtic knots can lead into ideas from knot theory; similarly the Shongo networks (Whitcombe and Donaldson 1988; Noyes 2007) observed in the Congo basin can be used as an introduction to the 'route inspection problem' studied as part of decision mathematics. These networks are designs that can be drawn in one movement without taking the pen away from the paper. You might like to try drawing the two designs in Figure 6.2 for yourself. Are all such designs able to be drawn in such a way? How might this be linked to the problem facing a council when they need to grit a network of roads as quickly and cheaply as possible?

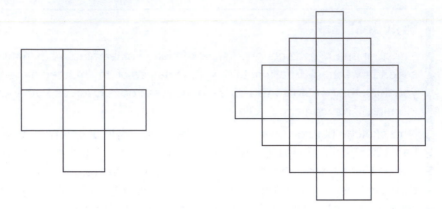

Figure 6.2 Two examples of Shongo networks

At other times, culturally embedded uses of mathematics can motivate the practice and application of a method. For instance, Islamic laws of inheritance can be used as a framework with which to practice the skills of calculating fractions and using ratios. One historical recording of this law is summarised in Joseph (1991: 319):

> when a woman dies her husband receives one-quarter of her estate, and the rest is divided among the children such that a son receives twice as much as a daughter. However, if a legacy is left to a stranger ... [the] stranger cannot receive more than one third of the estate without the permission of the natural heirs. If some of the natural heirs endorse such a legacy but others do not, those who do must between them pay, *pro rata*, out of their own shares, the amount by which the stranger's legacy exceeds one-third of the estate. In any case, the legacy to the stranger has to be paid before the rest is shared out among the natural heirs.

Although it can be time-consuming to research, evaluate and present mathematics from different cultures, it is a valuable addition to cross-curricular practice, and can serve to motivate the wider study of mathematics:

> In our increasingly culturally diverse classrooms, identifying for young people how their own cultural heritage has contributed to mathematical thinking would not be a bad thing. Recently a young Pakistani history teacher explained to me why she was leaving the profession: *the history she was teaching was not her history*. In a similar sense there might be some value in identifying and using mathematics from Africa, the Middle and Far East, and Asia.
>
> (Noyes 2007: 74)

Mathematics and religion

Some of the examples of mathematics offered above do not only have a historical and a cultural context, but also a religious one. Although the connection between mathematics and religion may not be immediately obvious to the modern reader, historically the two have been closely related, with mathematics supporting (and in some cases helping to make up) the world views of different cultures. In Greek mathematics, Pythagoras' teachings concern religious observance as much as mathematical structure, and he famously declared that 'all is number'. Plato proposed that the very structure of the universe was reflected in geometry when he associated the four elements of air, fire, water and earth with four of the five Platonic solids; he went on to speculate that the fifth solid, the dodecahedron, was used for the purpose of arranging the universe. There is a strong metaphysical flavour to much of the early history of mathematics.

Numbers would appear to play a significant role in many religions. For instance, although there is a large amount of interpretation involved in any reading of religious texts, certain numbers would appear to have some level of meaning in the Bible. As an example, consider the number seven: the creation story unfolds over seven days, there are seven feast days described in Leviticus, Jesus is quoted as instructing his followers to forgive 'seventy times seven' times, then has seven sayings on the cross, and in the book of Revelation there are seven churches, seven seals, seven trumpets and seven bowls. This theme is later picked up by the Christian church which features seven sacraments and talks of seven deadly sins. Similar lists can be constructed for other key numbers such as ten and twelve.

However, such associations are not always universal; in China the number seven is associated with death and tragedy. Conversely, the number 666, held by many Christians to be 'the number of the beast', is often displayed on the front of shops; the Chinese word for the number 6 is a homonym for the word 'flow', so the repetition 666 here signifies the idea of a smooth, problem-free time.

Although facts like these can be interesting, their use in the mathematics classroom is perhaps limited and they should be used carefully. Numerology in particular can be understood as being largely subjective; after all, there were also seven dwarfs! On the other hand, the idea of finding hidden meanings through the manipulation of numbers is a seductive one and it can lead to cross-curricular explorations in art and RE (Musto 2009).

A more obvious way that mathematics is connected to religious practice is in the use of geometry. Many religions use geometric patterns in their practice, and it is interesting to speculate why properties such as symmetry are so prevalent in religious iconography.

Rangoli patterns are colourful designs which are drawn by Hindus during the festival of Diwali to welcome the goddess Lakshmi into their homes. These patterns typically have four lines of symmetry, and have the potential to possess a number of different orders of rotational symmetry. Pupils can construct a Rangoli pattern in the classroom by drawing a square then lightly sketching in its four lines of symmetry. They then fill in one of the eight sections with their own design and then proceed to reflect it around the square.

Geometric designs also feature heavily in other religions; Islamic art, for example, has an extensive history that weaves religious beliefs together with mathematical ideals of pattern and order. One way in which these patterns might be seen to arise is through the Vedic square, an arrangement of numbers that became part of Islamic tradition via ancient Indian mathematics.

To create a Vedic square, draw a 9 × 9 grid and fill in the numbers from 1 to 9 along the top row and the leftmost column. To fill in the rest of the grid, take each square in turn. Multiply the number that is at the top of that column by the number that is to the far left of that row. If the number has more than one digit, add the digits together. To convert this pattern of numbers into a shape, choose a digit, for example '3', and then join together all of the squares that contain this digit in a manner of your own choosing. Figure 6.3, drawn from Metz (1991: 100–102) is provided below as an example, together with a demonstration of how this might be used to form a pattern.

Metz (1991) goes on to compare such patterns with those seen in Islamic art, and then links this method with more advanced construction techniques. It is impossible to do justice here to the variety and subtleties present in Islamic art, but this simple exercise does demonstrate how mathematical ideas can be embedded into religious art in a significant way.

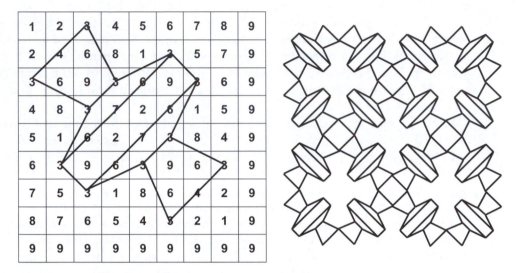

Figure 6.3 A pattern from a Vedic square.

Mathematics and RE

The discussion of mathematics alongside religion raises a challenging question: is there a sense in which mathematics can be thought to be spiritual? Although this might seem a strange question to ask, the National Curriculum does suggest that all subjects should contribute to a pupil's spiritual development. The previous edition of the National Curriculum was even more explicit, claiming that mathematics should promote 'spiritual development, through helping pupils obtain an insight into the infinite, and through explaining the underlying mathematical principles behind some of the beautiful natural forms and patterns in the world around us' (DfEE/QCA 1999: 8).

It is fair to say that a sense of the spiritual might inform a pupil's appreciation of mathematical concepts such as infinity or randomness. This might not be an explicit religious spirituality, but a less defined appreciation and awareness of the individual's place in the universe. Watson (1999) proposes that mathematics offers pupils the chance to develop their sense of wonder and wondering, and this could be seen as being 'spiritual' in some sense. This is a profound and sometimes controversial issue, but it is one which you might like to reflect upon.

> ## Reflective task
>
> To what extent do you think mathematics can be said to have a spiritual component? Have there been any occasions in your own mathematical experience where you have been particularly moved to wonder by a piece of mathematics? Do you think pupils are given the opportunity to have these sorts of experiences?

The discussion above has hopefully demonstrated that there is significant potential for developing cross-curricular activity that involves both mathematics and RE. The socially and culturally situated nature of mathematics as a discipline makes it inevitable that some elements of mathematics have been absorbed and integrated into religious belief systems. Whilst the use of these contexts in the mathematics classroom should be handled with care, they do provide another opportunity to demonstrate the authentic and profound role that mathematics plays in the modern world.

There are also a number of contexts that are similar to those used in the previous chapter to explore ideas from citizenship and geography. Statistics can be listed to map the growth and decline of different religions over time, and graphs can be constructed to compare the proportions of adherents to different religions in two different countries. However, whilst such activities are both valid and useful, it is important not to forego the wider opportunities that RE offers to develop pupils' sense of wonder and their appreciation of mathematics.

Mathematics and art

Some of the examples offered above have begun to touch on a further curriculum area: art. However, it is important at this point to remember that the definition of 'cross-curricular' offered in Chapter 1 requires an authentic sensitivity towards, and synthesis of, the subjects involved. Although an activity might be engaging and appealing for use in the classroom, is it genuinely mathematical, and is it truly art? (Hawkin 1994) These are problematic questions with no easy answers, and they involve a fuller discussion of philosophy and aesthetics than is allowed here. Nevertheless, when planning cross-curricular activities in this area it is worth keeping in mind that a mathematics teacher's view of what qualifies as art and an art teacher's view of what mathematics consists of may both be lacking. It is also valuable to remember to interrogate any proposed cross-curricular activities and question whether and how they will benefit the pupils' understanding in each of the subject areas involved.

The stereotypical characters of art and mathematics are very different, leading Davis (1994) to ask whether combining these two subjects is akin to putting 'cold callipers against warm flesh'. However, he goes on to claim that 'the relationship between art and mathematics is a very rich field for inquiry and speculation' (p. 166). It is certainly true that the history of the relationship between these two fields is rich and varied. During periods such as the Renaissance the arts and sciences were more closely connected, and famed thinkers such as Leonardo da Vinci were proficient in both areas. Conversely, there are significant periods, such as the present, where there is a substantial perceived divide, and at school pupils are generally encouraged towards either the sciences or the arts. The final part of this chapter will put forward the case that there is substantial opportunity to reconnect mathematics and art through cross-curricular activities, and offer some examples of how this might be done.

Proportion and perspective

Two key topics that link mathematics and art are proportion and perspective. Albarn (1991: 21) suggests that these ideas have both arisen out of a deeper search for meaning: 'proportion, number, ratio-geometry, perspective, rhythm and harmony all derive from mankind's early searches for a Grand Design, a pattern that should give shape to our experience and aid our survival.'

This search for relationships and patterns has led to certain rules being established for paintings and sculptures. The Greeks held that the idealised human form was eight heads tall, although many 'rules of thumb' now place the value closer to seven heads. The eyes are traditionally drawn at the mid-height of the head, and the width of the base of the nose is approximately the same as the width of each eye. Perhaps the most obvious example of proportion being used in art is Leonardo da Vinci's *Vitruvian Man*, a study of the male figure based on the proportions given by the Roman writer Vitruvius.

These principles of bodily proportion can be explored in the mathematics classroom. Da Vinci noted that the length of a man's hand is one-tenth of his height – this theory can be tested using the pupils as a convenience sample; experiments like this can lead into valuable discussions about accuracy, and possibly even how being at different stages of puberty can affect the proportions of the human body. Another exercise is to test pupils' faces for symmetry; digitally photograph a willing volunteer's face, cut the image vertically down the middle and reflect one half of the face to create a perfectly symmetrical image. Does the 'symmetrical' pupil look markedly different? Do famous actors and actresses have perfectly symmetrical faces? Is perfect symmetry beautiful, or does asymmetry add character?

One instance of proportion that has been of particular interest to both mathematicians and artists is the golden ratio, approximately 1:1.618. This ratio is connected to many mathematical topics, including the Fibonacci sequence, the lengths of lines joining the vertices of a regular pentagon and Penrose tiling. In terms of aesthetics, the golden ratio gives rise to what is known as the 'golden rectangle', which is held to be the most aesthetically pleasing shape of rectangle. Both the golden ratio and the golden rectangle have been used extensively in art (by artists such as Dali and Mondrian) and architecture (including the Parthenon and buildings designed by the Swiss-French architect Corbusier). There are also a number of other claimed 'sightings' of the golden ratio in other, more surprising fields: Weiss and Weiss (2003) appear to show in experiments that the golden ratio is present in the way that the brain codes information, whilst Coldea *et al*. (2010) report that the golden ratio is also present at the atomic level in the magnetic resonances of cobalt niobate atoms. Not all occurrences of the golden ratio are supported by robust evidence, but it is certainly a proportional relationship which seems to occur curiously often, and it could form the basis of an interesting cross-curricular investigation that moved from mathematics to art and beyond.

Another key feature in the construction of many pieces of art is perspective. Perspective is essentially a visual illusion that encourages the viewer to perceive an element of depth in a flat painting or drawing. The most common and easily understood use of perspective involves vanishing points. In this method lines that emanate from a fixed point on the page (a vanishing point) are understood to be parallel in real-life. The choice between one, two or three vanishing points is usually meaningful, as each style of perspective focuses the attention of the audience in a different way.

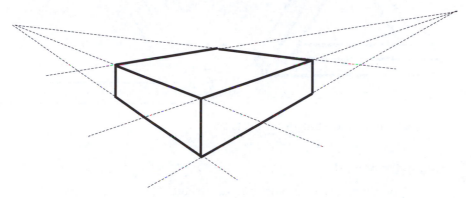

Figure 6.4 A cuboid represented using two-point perspective.

From a geometrical point of view there are a number of challenging questions that can be asked: for instance, will a line segment in the real world always be represented as a line segment on the page, or can it ever appear curved? What will happen to a circle when it is drawn in perspective? The principles of perspective also offer pupils an additional way with which to represent and explore the properties of three dimensional shapes.

Some artists have deliberately used distorted forms of perspective in their paintings. One of the most famous examples of this is Holbein's *The Ambassadors* which contains a strange diagonal shape in the bottom of the painting. When the painting is viewed from a particular angle this turns out to be a skull. This principle could be used as the basis for a practical activity (Gardner 1988: 97–109). Distorted perspective, or anamorphosis, is also used in cinematography when moving between images with widescreen and standard aspect ratios.

Perspective can also be recruited in the construction of illusion. In the 1950s, the English mathematician Roger Penrose devised and popularised a peculiar shape now known as the 'Penrose triangle' or the 'impossible triangle'. This shape appears at first glance to be a solid object but is in fact impossible to construct in real space. It can, however, be constructed by pupils in the classroom, using three nested equilateral triangles as the basis of the drawing (Figure 6.5). 'Impossible' objects feature extensively in the works of the famed Dutch artist M.C. Escher: impossible triangles form the basis of the lithograph print *Waterfall* and a set of endless stairs constructed by Penrose found their way into the work *Ascending and Descending*. Escher held a keen interest in mathematics and many explicit geometric elements find their way into his works; for instance, the two towers in *Waterfall* are topped by a stellation of a rhombic dodecahedron and a compound of three cubes.

Mathematics continues to help artists work with perspective today; in computer graphics linear algebra techniques such as matrix multiplication and vector methods are used to create the illusion of a three-dimensional image.

Figure 6.5 An impossible triangle and how to draw it.

Geometry and art

The relationship between geometry and art is both complex and subtle; it has been asked on a number of occasions whether we can tell exactly where one ends and another begins. This semantic blurring is particularly salient in the case of artists such as Mondrian. Piet Mondrian was a Dutch painter whose works were often based around a grid of vertical and horizontal lines, with rectangular regions coloured using the three primary colours. Geometric elements are also heavily featured in the works of artists such as Frank Stella, and 'op art' artists, such as Bridget Riley, who are concerned with creating illusions through the use of geometric forms. The work of any of these artists could provide a starting point for a cross-curricular project.

The artist M.C. Escher, discussed above, used the idea of tessellation in much of his art, tiling the plane with copies of the same image (Jones 1991). Work such as *Circle Limit IV* takes the idea of tiling the hyperbolic plane and displays a sophisticated grasp of non-Euclidean geometry. When exploring the concept of tessellation with pupils it is worthwhile showing them some of these images, and encouraging them to develop more sophisticated tessellations of their own. This can be done by starting with a shape that is known to tessellate, removing a section from this shape then fixing it back onto the shape elsewhere so that the resultant shape tessellates (Figure 6.6). The nature of tessellation allows for further mathematical discussion about transformations, particularly translations and rotations (Britton 2003).

The idea of tessellation in art has been carried on and developed by the contemporary artist, Peter Raedschelders. Figure 6.7 shows how scaled versions of the same shape can be used to make a tessellation with self-similar overtones.

Sometimes the same piece of mathematics can give rise to two very different pictures. Both of the pictures in Figure 6.8 were based around the same pattern of hyperbolas shown in the centre. You might like to show these pictures to your pupils and ask them what mathematics they can see. How are the pictures similar? How are they different?

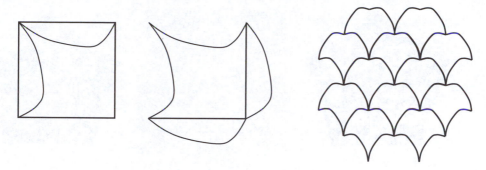

Figure 6.6 Developing more complex shapes for tessellation.

Figure 6.7 *Stegosaurus* by Peter Raedschelders.

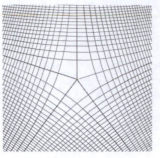

Figure 6.8 *Five Snakes* and *Tropical Fish* by Peter Raedschelders.

Modern developments in mathematics continue to inspire artists, and fields such as fractal geometry continue to blur the distinction between the two subjects. This blurring is evident in the mathematics classroom whenever pupils explore patterns for themselves and create visual representations that cause them to express a sense of wonder and aesthetic appreciation. These opportunities can arise more easily if pupils have the chance to explore geometry using computers, experimenting with REPEAT commands in LOGO, or exploring polar rose curves (curves of the form $r = \cos(k\theta)$ where k is a constant) with computer programs such as Autograph. This discussion has only begun to consider some of the many ways that art can be brought into the mathematics classroom in a productive, cross-curricular way, and has barely touched on three-dimensional forms of art or architecture. However, it serves to demonstrate that the two subjects do have significant links which are a far cry from being 'cold callipers on warm flesh'.

Practical task

Magic Monkeys by Peter Raedschelders is a tessellation made up of 16 groups of four colours of monkeys; moving clockwise from the top left these are black, brown, dark grey and light grey. However, this tessellation also hides a super-magic square.

- Consider the picture as a 4 x 4 grid, where each square contains one monkey of each colour. If a monkey has its eyes closed it gets 0 points. However, if it has its eyes open it is awarded some points: a black monkey gets 8 points, a light grey monkey gets 4 points, a dark grey monkey gets 2 points and a brown monkey gets 1 point.

- Draw a 4 x 4 grid and write in the score for each cell. Check that this gives you a magic square.

- Now look at any one of the 4 x 4 squares around the edge of the picture. Add up the values of the cells that correspond to the black squares. Why is this picture a super-magic square?

- How do the highlighted patterns in the corners tell you which monkeys have their eyes open?

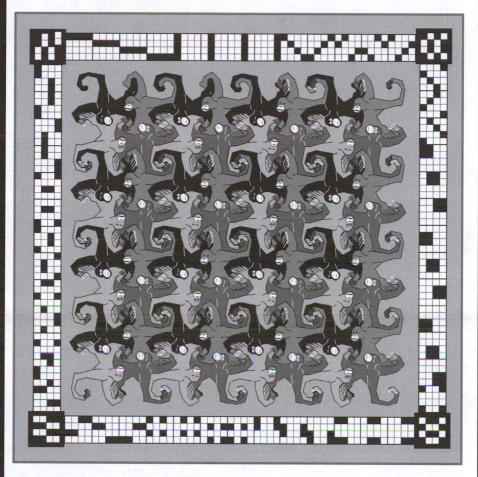

Figure 6.9 *Magic Monkeys* by Peter Raedschelders

Summary

The three subjects considered in this chapter are all very different in their characters; however, they have been brought together here as they all offer pupils a chance to gain a different perspective on what constitutes mathematics. Exploring mathematics through the lens of history shows it to be a developing, human discipline. Seeing how mathematics is reflected in different religions suggests that there is, and always has been, something profound about the mathematical experience. Finally, using art as the basis for recreational mathematics reminds us of the aesthetic aspect of the subject.

Cross-curricular activity is ideally designed and carried out to benefit the component subjects. Many of the examples offered in this chapter fulfil this brief in a substantial way, not only developing pupils' understanding of the mathematical concepts involved, but also informing their relationship with the subject itself. This is another reason why cross-curricular practice is a valuable, if not a vital tool in the presentation of mathematics.

Professional Standards for QTS

This chapter will help you meet the following Q standards: Q8, Q10, Q14, Q18, Q19.

Professional Standards for Teachers

This chapter will help you meet the following core standards: C8, C10, C15, C18, C19.

Further reading

www.mathsisgoodforyou.com
> This website, written and collated by Dr. Snezana Lawrence, holds a plethora of ideas and classroom resources based around the history of mathematics.

Jones, L. (ed.) (1991) *Teaching Mathematics and Art.*
> This edited book draws together chapters which examine some of the many aspects of the relationship between mathematics and art. It also contains a good number of activities which are suitable for the secondary mathematics classroom.

Procedures, symbolism and modelling: mathematics and ICT, business studies and economics

The previous chapters of this book have begun to demonstrate how fundamental processes such as constructing and following an argument stretch across the curricula of a large number of subjects, and how mathematics often plays a central role in these processes. This chapter goes on to consider another such process: designing and following instructions, and demonstrates how a cross-curricular presentation of the idea of an algorithm can help pupils to develop this important skill.

The subject of ICT, however, offers more to the mathematics teacher than just a context for constructing flowcharts. One of the most challenging tasks that a mathematics teacher faces is how to motivate and encourage children to learn their subject. This dilemma is particularly pronounced in the case of algebra, and many pupils leave school without a clear understanding of either the purpose of algebra, or even what algebra actually *is*. Once again, cross-curricular teaching and learning can begin to provide a solution to this problem. Subject areas such as ICT, business studies and economics are ideal arenas within which pupils can apply algebraic methods and extend their own understanding in a significant and meaningful way. The use of formulae in spreadsheets, for example, can help pupils move from a syntactic to a semantic understanding of algebra, developing a more flexible sense of the meaning that lies behind the symbols.

All three subjects also provide a fertile ground for pupils to practice the skills of mathematical modelling, representing real-life problems in mathematical ways so as to better understand them and reach appropriate solutions. This practice is not only an increasingly prominent part of many qualifications but a fundamental component of modern applied mathematics which could benefit many pupils in their future study and employment.

Key objectives

By the end of this chapter, you will have:

- Investigated some of the links between the subjects of mathematics, ICT, business studies and economics

- Considered how the idea of an algorithm is common to mathematics, ICT and many other subjects

- Briefly examined how pupils' algebraic understanding and reasoning develops over time

- Considered how spreadsheets can be used to challenge and develop pupils' use of symbols in algebra

- Explored the process of mathematical modelling, and seen how it can be used in scenarios drawn from a number of curriculum areas

Mathematics and ICT

If a teacher from twenty years ago was to walk into a contemporary school, one of the first things they would notice would be the way that technology is now integrated into the classroom. This is particularly true in the case of mathematics classrooms, where graphical calculators, voting pods, subject-specific websites, interactive whiteboards and a number of specialist packages and activities have all been used to great effect (Johnston-Wilder and Pimm 2005; Oldknow and Taylor 2003). However, in some cases the use of ICT to support the teaching and learning of mathematics has overshadowed the opportunities which ICT offers as a subject in its own right.

In light of the cross-curricular focus of this book, this chapter will not consider ICT resources, such as dynamic geometry software, which have been specially designed for the mathematics classroom. It will focus instead on cases where the ICT content is itself central to the pupils' learning. There are many such cases, since the relationship between the subject areas of mathematics and ICT is particularly strong; indeed, it is not uncommon to find teachers in secondary schools who have some experience of teaching both subjects. Ideas of structure, relationships and problem solving are fundamental to both subjects, and their relevance means that both subjects are considered to contain 'functional' skills in the current National Curriculum (QCA 2007). There is also substantial specific overlap in the skills and content taught in both subjects.

Bits, bytes and binary representations

Mathematics is present at even the most basic level of data storage. Computers most often use binary notation to store information in an electronic format. The binary system consists of two states, 0 and 1, so the computer only has to distinguish between two levels of voltage in order to interpret stored data. If the computer was to use the decimal system, it would have to accurately distinguish between ten levels of voltage, and there would be a much greater potential for error.

The characters that make up this page of writing have been translated into binary using a system known as ASCII, or the American Standard Code for Information Interchange, which allocates a numerical code to each character. For example, when I type the capital letter 'M', the computer knows this symbol has the ASCII code of '77'. This is then changed into binary and stored on my hard drive as 1001101, since $77 = 1 \times 2^6 + 0 \times 2^5 + 0 \times 2^4 + 1 \times 2^3 + 1 \times 2^2 + 0 \times 2^1 + 1 \times 2^0$. The ASCII encoding system can be accessed directly in some word processing programs – in

Microsoft Word, for example, holding down the Alt key and typing '77' on the number pad produces the 'M' character.

This system gives rise to a number of interesting questions and challenges that can be considered in the mathematics classroom: can the pupils encode their own first names in seven-bit binary code? (ASCII tables are readily available online to help with this conversion.) How many different characters can be represented using a combination of seven 1s and 0s? Why did the developers of the ASCII originally decide on a seven-bit code? Nowadays, binary digits, or bits, are often combined into groups of eight, known as bytes. What role does the eighth digit play?

As the quantity of information being considered increases, new units are used that link to the mathematical topic of measures. However, it is important to note that there is a slight discrepancy in the way that prefixes are used. It is often assumed that 'kilobyte' (Kb) means one thousand bytes, in the same way that 'kilometre' means one thousand metres. This is almost correct; however, since the bit and byte system is based around powers of 2, a kilobyte is actually 2^{10}, or 1,024 bytes. Similarly, a megabyte (Mb) is equal to 2^{20} bytes, and a gigabyte (Gb) hard drive holds 2^{30} bytes of information, which is 7.4 per cent larger than you might expect from the usual meaning of 'giga'.

At the time of writing it is possible to purchase a terabyte (2^{40} byte) hard drive, and petabyte (2^{50} byte) hard drives are being touted as imminent. You might like to explore with the pupils why the size of available hard drives is increasing so rapidly – could they gather some data to find out which types of files take up the most space on a computer hard drive? Could they then use their results to justify the need for a terabyte hard drive?

Another interesting avenue of investigation is to examine how hard disk size has increased over time, and to make predictions about the size of hard disks in the future. A number of technologists and futurists have attempted to do exactly this, and there are a number of laws, such as Moore's Law, which suggest that the power of computers is growing exponentially. An exploration of laws such as these can involve mathematical techniques such as logarithms and geometric series, as well as giving rise to some higher-order questions: what factors might limit continued exponential growth? Can 'laws' such as these be understood better as observations or self-fulfilling prophecies?

Bases other than binary are used elsewhere in ICT. The hexadecimal system (base 16) uses the digits 0 to 9 followed by A to F. This system is used to specify colours in HTML, the language of website programming. Each colour is represented by a six digit string, RRGGBB, where RR dictates the amount of red, GG the amount of green, and BB the amount of blue. 'Dark Orchid', for instance, is represented by 9A32CD – a lot of red and blue, but not much green results in a specific shade of purple. Questions that arise from this system of notation could include: which colours are represented by 000000 and FFFFFF? Can you design a code that would give rise to a turquoise colour? How many different gradations of red can be represented by this system? How many different colours can be formed in total?

Programs and algorithms

Mathematics is still very much in evidence when we move from the level of information to the programs themselves. For instance Internet search engines use Boolean logic, which has many notational and structural links to the mathematics curriculum. Different search engines have different syntaxes, but Google infers a logical AND from whitespace; so typing in *"maths" "ict"* will search for maths AND ict, then report the intersection of the sets of results that would arise from searching for *maths* and *ict* individually. Other syntaxes are more explicit: to search for either or both terms being present in a web page, Google requires a logical OR command, *"maths" OR "ict"*, whereas a logical NOT is represented by a minus sign, *"maths" –"ict"*. Boolean logic is also employed by many database programs in order to perform queries. The ideas being used in these programs can help to illustrate topics such as Venn diagrams, or be connected to the notation used when exploring the probability of multiple events, such as $P(A \cap B)$ to mean the intersection of sets A and B.

Mathematics is also used extensively by e-mail software. The last chapter considered some historical examples of cryptography, and this theme can be carried through into the present day by looking at how mathematics is used to encode and decode e-mails to protect privacy. One popular method, RSA public-key cryptography, involves multiplying two large prime numbers together to form a very large composite number. The prime numbers are used to encode an e-mail, which is then sent together with the composite number. It can then only be decoded by someone who has access to the original prime numbers. Anyone who isn't the intended recipient would have to find the prime factors through exhaustive methods which, in the case of very long numbers, would take many years (Singh 2000). However, as the processing speed of computers increases, the time it would take to 'crack' such a code decreases, and this fact motivates the search for ever larger prime numbers. At the time of writing, the largest known prime is 12,978,189 digits long, and the last 14 record primes have all been Mersenne primes, prime numbers of the form 2^p-1 where p is also a prime number. Many of these were found by an organisation called GIMPS (the Great Internet Mersenne Prime Search) which uses collaborative computing to test numbers more quickly.

Internet cryptography is a fertile area for cross-curricular investigation: you might choose to look at the development of cryptography through time, go into some detail about the number theory behind the encryption algorithms, explore how computing power has developed over time and forced more complex encryption procedures, challenge pupils in groups to find the largest prime number they can, or even set up a classroom computer to join GIMPS. In addition, the University of Southampton runs a national cipher challenge each year (www.cipher.maths.soton.ac.uk) which can be used as either a classroom resource or a source of enrichment materials for eager cryptographers.

Mathematics is also used to help identify and remove 'spam' e-mails. Spam e-mails are a growing problem, and reports have suggested that between 85 per cent and 95 per cent of sent e-mails are unwanted by the recipient. It is therefore important for mail handling programs to have the ability to filter out the majority of these messages. Some filters use language recognition, taking out e-mails written in a language other than the user's own. However, this method is not ideal for multi-national companies, and also still allows through many unwanted messages. Another filter technique is to block any messages that contain words that appear to suggest that the content is inappropriate. This filter can also be circumvented, however, by rewriting words in novel ways, such as *w0rd$*. If a filter tries to recognise parts of words to combat this problem it can reject many valid messages; I know of one school where the e-mail filter rejects any messages which include the word "analysis" in the title!

A possible solution to this has come from the field of Bayesian statistics, which involves the study of conditional probability. The conditional probability of A given B, or $P(A \mid B)$, is the probability of an event A given that we know another event B has already happened. Bayesian spam filters 'learn' over time, calculating both the observed frequencies of spam e-mails and particular words, and also the conditional probabilities of words such as 'lottery' being present in messages that you have identified as being spam. It can then calculate the overall probability that an e-mail containing that word is spam using Bayes' theorem:

$$P(Spam \mid "Lottery") = \frac{P("Lottery" \mid Spam)P(Spam)}{P("Lottery")}$$

These probabilities are constantly adjusted as the user gives feedback to the filter, and so over time the filter becomes attuned to the individual user's activities. Bayesian probability is also used widely in other fields: neuroscientists have used it to model the way the nervous system interprets and adjusts to different sensory inputs, and astronomers sometimes use a Bayesian algorithm known as a Bayesian Kepler periodogram to detect planets that lie outside of our solar system.

What many of these ideas have in common is the idea of an algorithm, an ordered set of instructions that is followed as part of a procedure or action. Flowcharts and algorithms are explicitly considered in ICT as part of the process of software design, and they can also feature in supporting documentation. For instance, a flowchart might show the algorithm a control system in an automated greenhouse follows when it interrogates a sensor in order to decide whether the temperature is too low, and what action it takes based on this reading. Algorithms also play a key role in many computer programming languages.

Algorithms and flowcharts also feature throughout the mathematics curriculum. Whilst not all schemes and syllabuses explicitly teach using these terms, many do, and all implicitly require pupils to be able to follow an algorithm. For instance, the column method of adding a pair of numbers together is most often taught as an algorithm (see Figure 7.1), as is the procedure for adding two fractions together. Flowcharts can also provide an excellent way of communicating iterative or recursive procedures.

The topic of algorithms is dominant in A-level option modules that are focused on decision, or discrete mathematics, wherein pupils learn algorithms for optimising revenue, finding a critical path when managing a project and identifying the shortest path that connects two points in a network.

The idea of an algorithm is powerfully cross-curricular, and moving between subjects can reinforce pupils' understanding of what an algorithm is and help to develop their ability to deconstruct a process in a thorough and logical way. As we become an increasingly technological society these skills will become more important in the workplace, not only for those working to design technology, but for anyone who has to use it in an efficient, safe, and reliable way.

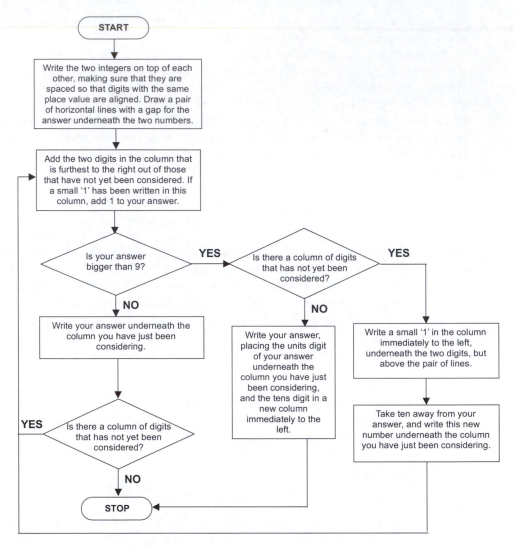

Figure 7.1 A flowchart of the column addition algorithm.

Reflective task

To develop pupils' ability to work with algorithms, it is useful to give them practice at both applying and designing their own algorithms. However, it is also important to give them the opportunity to compare different algorithms that have been designed for the same purpose, and reflect on the range and limitations of different algorithms.

Think of a particular set or group of pupils, and then look over the list of examples given below. Which of these algorithms could you use to develop these pupils' higher-order thinking in the ways described above? How might you use these algorithms in the classroom? Can you think of any other examples of your own which might be introduced in a lesson?

- how a pupil might multiply a pair of two-digit numbers;
- how a pupil might use the quadratic formula;
- how a computer might sort a list of numbers from smallest to largest;
- how to classify triangles;
- how an entomologist might classify a new species of insect;
- how a ferry operator might load a group of differently sized vehicles onto a passenger ferry;
- how a traffic light might 'decide' when to switch between colours.

ICT offers many other contexts which might be integrated into the mathematics classroom. The last digits of barcodes and ISBN codes, for example, are often check digits calculated using modular arithmetic. These built-in redundancy checks are an immediate example of how mathematics surrounds pupils in their every day lives, and the calculations used could form the basis of a classroom activity. There is also some direct overlap between mathematics and ICT, although it should be noted that this can sometimes involve different terminology. For instance, in mathematics pupils are required to design questionnaires, whilst in ICT they have to design data capture forms. Both tasks need the pupil to distinguish between qualitative and quantitative data, and both require some consideration of question phrasing, bias, and appropriate choices of response boxes.

Finally, there are also other shared processes that can be linked together by the cross-curricular practitioner. In ICT students learn about the 'life cycle' of an information system or piece of software. This begins with identifying and analysing the problem, and designing a solution. This is then implemented, tested and evaluated. The evaluation feeds back into a new cycle, wherein any problems are addressed. The system life cycle has clear connections to the data handling cycle taught in mathematics, as well as more general iterative approaches to mathematical problem solving.

Spreadsheets

The discussion above has demonstrated that the subjects of mathematics and ICT have a definite and extensive overlap both in terms of content and in terms of the skills they demand and develop. This connection is particularly strong in the case of spreadsheets. Spreadsheet programs usually incorporate specific commands which perform mathematical operations; Microsoft Excel, for instance, includes the commands SUM, ROUND, GCD (greatest common divisor, the same as highest common factor), AVERAGE (arithmetic mean), STDEV (standard deviation) and PEARSON (for Pearson's product-moment correlation coefficient). The structure of a spreadsheet and its ability to hold a number of cells of data allows pupils to explore the properties of these mathematical commands in a direct way. For instance, you might set up the numbers 1,

2, 3, 4 and 5 in the top row of cells, and beneath calculate the AVERAGE and STDEV of these cells. Can the pupils alter the values in the cells to find a set of values that has a mean that is twice as large, but has the same standard deviation? Can they find a set of numbers that has the same mean, but a standard deviation that is twice as big as before?

These sorts of activities can encourage pupils to explore the mathematical concepts involved with much less fear of failure; the computer is now offering feedback, not the teacher, and there is no permanent record of any failed attempts. However, the spreadsheet is still largely being used as an sophisticated calculator. Spreadsheets have more to offer than just this, and can give rise to a number of opportunities for learning about algebra.

The development of algebraic thinking

It is a common observation that pupils find it difficult to master algebra. It is undoubtable that some of this difficulty stems from the highly abstracted way in which algebra is often introduced in the classroom:

> For many students, the whole subject of algebra frequently becomes associated at a very early stage with tasks which appear to lack any meaning or serve any obvious useful purpose. This naturally leads to failure and distaste… Meaning can only be imparted alongside purpose: this strange new language needs to explain things and to solve problems that are significant to the learner. Students need to see it as helping to make some tasks simpler rather than complicating simple tasks that they can already do in other ways.
>
> (French 2002: 26–27)

Alongside these concerns, it is also important to recognise that mastery of algebra requires a significant amount of cognitive development and practice. Whilst it is arguably a natural human instinct to generalise and specialise as part of interpreting the surrounding environment, the processes of rigour and logic are not as instinctive, and it is certainly not fair to expect pupils to naturally connect their informal ideas of generalisation to one particular system of notation that is based on hundreds of years of agreed convention.

One of the largest scale surveys of children's understandings of algebra is reported in Küchemann (1981), part of the Concepts in Secondary Mathematics and Science (CSMS) study. This study found that children understood letters in algebra problems in six distinct ways (p. 104). These were:

- Letter evaluated
- Letter not used
- Letter as an object
- Letter as a specific unknown
- Letter as a generalised number
- Letter as a variable

Although these understandings are not intended as a strict hierarchy, they do reflect some measure of progress.

Reflective task

Think back to your experiences with pupils learning algebra. Which of these six interpretations of letters have you seen pupils use? How might these different understandings manifest themselves as difficulties when solving different types of problem?

The following three-part question was one of those given to 14-year-old pupils as part of the CSMS study (p. 106). The results hint at some of the different ways in which pupils can understand letters.

If a + b = 43,
what is a + b + 2 worth?
(97 per cent correct)

If n - 246 = 762,
what is n - 247 worth?
(74 per cent correct)

If e + f = 8, what is
e + f + g worth?
(41 per cent correct)

Although these results can be interpreted in a number of different ways, the drop in performance between the first two questions suggests that many pupils are reliant on the order of the symbols given. The large drop in performance on the final question suggests that many pupils have a tendency to try and see through the letters and treat them as specific numbers; less than half were able to interpret the 'g' in a sufficiently general way and give the correct answer of 8 + g.

This brief discussion has already suggested that there is a need for pupils to use algebra in a purposeful way that encourages them to move from a syntactic understanding of algebra to a semantic one; moving from seeing algebra as a system of symbols to a representation of relationships. One way of achieving this is through the use of spreadsheets and modelling in the mathematics classroom. Spreadsheet-based tasks can help pupils to better understand both the purpose and utility of algebra (Ainley *et al.* 2005).

Teaching mathematics through spreadsheets

Algebra is fundamental to the nature of spreadsheet packages; arguably it is the ability of such packages to deal with algebraic expressions and relationships that moves them beyond simply being programs that draw tables and graphs. This same capability can be used to develop pupils' emerging algebraic understanding in a way that pencil and paper methods cannot. Rojano found that pupils who used spreadsheets in mathematical problem solving had the chance to develop their thinking in a qualitatively different way to those who did not:

> The awareness of the interdependent relationship between unknowns, the choice of an unknown for variation, and the work itself on an unknown quantity in order to find its numerical value, subject to the constraints of the problem, form the basis of the substantial differences between the variation of the unknown in the spreadsheet method and the informal strategy of trial and error.
>
> (Rojano 1996: 145)

Arguably, the way that spreadsheet packages connect meaning to symbolism means that pupils can see more clearly beyond the notation, and also encourages them to develop partly formed ideas through experimentation. For instance, to set up a 'profit' cell, a pupil can enter an equals sign, then click on the 'income' cell, enter a subtraction sign and click on the 'costs' cell. The meaning is more readily apparent at each stage and there is more support and scaffolding then there would be in writing an equation 'dry'. As noted above, the spreadsheet also serves to produce a virtual environment where pupils can try things out for themselves and gain instant feedback, with little or no fear of failure.

There are limits to the ways that a spreadsheet can, and should be used in the mathematics classroom: it is not fully algebraic, and the 'grammar' used by spreadsheets is different from that of standard algebra, so there is still a definite need for pupils to work with conventional forms of symbols. However, when used well spreadsheets have the potential to produce substantial benefits:

> using a spreadsheet, which by itself would lead students to solve problems by trial and error, under the attentive guidance of a teacher can lead them… to understand what solving an equation means, even before being able to handle equations… to introduce generalisation, abstraction and synthesis, which are fundamental cognitive abilities in mathematics… [and] to become aware of the nature of algebra by comparing, as a metacognitive activity, different problem solving methodologies, such as arithmetic, algebra and spreadsheets.
>
> (Dettori *et al*. 2001: 207)

Furthermore, since pupils are taught how to use spreadsheets in ICT, it would be remiss to ignore this fact and not encourage the pupils to connect their experiences in ICT to their developing appreciation of algebra. This can take place through spreadsheet tasks that have clear links to the mathematics curriculum.

Mathematical spreadsheet tasks

One way to develop pupils' appreciation of letters or cells as variables is through experimentation with relative and absolute referencing. Relative referencing is when a spreadsheet formula is connected to a cell specified through its relative position. For example, if you were to place a '1' in the cell A1, write the formula '=A1+2' underneath and then copy this formula down, each time the formula would update itself, becoming '=A2+2', '=A3+2' and so on, and the resulting list of numbers would be the odd numbers. Absolute referencing, on the other hand, always refers back to the same cell. Using the common '$' form of absolute referencing notation, we could write '=A1+2'. This formula would not change if it was copied down, and we would end up with a '1' followed by a column of '3's.

In both cases all of the values in the column will change whenever the initial reference is altered. Some spreadsheet packages have special functions that can help pupils make sense of these types of referencing; for instance, clicking on a cell and pressing F2 in Microsoft Excel highlights the cells that contribute to the selected cell in different colours.

Cell referencing can be used to generate sequences; the first example above is equivalent to generating a term-by-term sequence. One possible activity that is based around this starts with the teacher presenting pupils with an A4 sheet filled with numbers. Each column is a sequence of integers: the first few are linear sequences, but as you move towards the right the sheet introduces the square numbers, the triangular numbers and the Fibonacci numbers. The pupils are then challenged to reproduce this sheet and print it out by the end of the lesson. A similar activity involves challenging pupils to create a 10 × 10 times table grid by filling in the fewest cells possible and copying formulae across and down as appropriate.

Another activity based around cell referencing is to challenge pupils to create a spreadsheet that demonstrates what happens to the graph of $y = mx + c$ when the values of m and c change. Although there is specialist software that can graph algebraic expressions, pupils can benefit from explicitly developing their own piece of software as they are forced to explore the underlying structure of the mathematics for themselves. This way of using ICT is resonant with the constructionist principles discussed in Chapter 4. At the same time, the pupils will come across a number of problems that require them to improve their ICT knowledge; for instance, in order to see the effect of shifting the gradient properly they will have to fix the range of the axes. Pupils who are more experienced with spreadsheets might also go on to incorporate embedded spinners to change the values of m and c, as shown in Figure 7.2 below.

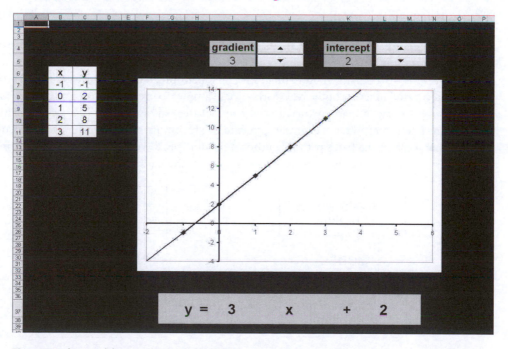

Figure 7.2 A spreadsheet to draw the graph of $y = mx + c$.

Spreadsheets can be invaluable tools of exploration and calculation in a number of other areas of mathematics. For instance, trial and improvement calculations can be carried out at speed and represented graphically, with calculated points getting closer to a target 'line'. Most spreadsheets also include the capacity to generate random numbers; through a formula such as $=1 + INT(RAND()*6)$ it is possible to utilise this facility to simulate the rolling of a regular, six-sided die. This can then be repeated to simulate large numbers of trials and explore probability and randomness (Johnston-Wilder 2005: 117–119).

In each of these activities, pupils' ICT knowledge should develop alongside pupils' understanding of the mathematics involved, through using a larger number of spreadsheet functions in increasingly complex ways. There is also scope for pupils who are well versed in ICT to write macros to perform common mathematical procedures. However, it should be remembered that spreadsheets are only one part of the ICT curriculum, and pupils should be encouraged to reflect upon their use of ICT in a more general way. What are the advantages and limitations of using a spreadsheet to represent these mathematical contexts? If they have designed their own spreadsheet or piece of software to solve a mathematical problem, does it fulfil the needs outlined in the brief? How could they improve it in the future? By asking questions such as these, we can help to develop tasks into more genuinely cross-curricular activities.

The discussion so far has illustrated how spreadsheets can be useful tools for performing calculations, developing some elements of algebraic thinking and exploring certain mathematical ideas. The next part of this chapter will go on to demonstrate how spreadsheets can also play an important role in introducing mathematical modelling into the classroom.

Mathematical modelling

At first glance, the process of mathematical modelling seems fairly straightforward to explain and understand: a real-life problem is simplified and expressed in a mathematical form. This mathematical approximation is then manipulated to produce a solution which is interpreted in terms of the real world. For example, to predict the path of a ball thrown through the air, a mathematician might model the ball as a particle, choose to ignore factors such as wind resistance and spin, and use techniques from mechanics to calculate the parabola of the ball's path from the angle and speed with which the ball is thrown. They could then use their model to predict where the ball would land.

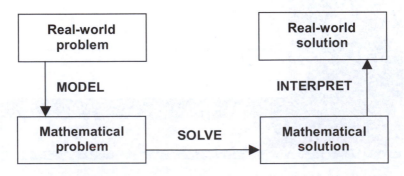

Figure 7.3 The process of mathematical modelling.

However, behind this simple diagram lies a plethora of difficult questions. Most immediately, when does a 'real-life' problem become a mathematical model? Beare (1997: 1) draws a useful distinction by considering the purpose of the mathematics: 'Real life problems in mathematics courses are subservient to mathematical understanding. The mathematics in a mathematical model, on the other hand, is subservient to promoting understanding of some aspect of real life.'

If we accept this definition it becomes apparent that modelling is profoundly cross-curricular. However, this distinction raises further questions about pedagogy. If modelling only takes place when the mathematics is subservient to a real-life situation, can authentic mathematical modelling be conducted in the classroom, where the focus is on teaching and learning? If it can, should it be taught as a separate skill, or developed in parallel with other mathematical concepts and techniques? How might the skill of modelling be assessed in a valid and reliable way? What might modelling look like at different levels of schooling?

These are difficult questions, which are discussed in depth elsewhere (for example, Blum *et al.* 2007). It is already evident, though, that there are a number of parallels between these issues and those surrounding functional mathematics, and some of the qualifications discussed in Chapter 1, as well as more general cross-curricular approaches to teaching mathematics. What is certain at this stage is that the skills of being able to identify the salient features of a real-life problem, express them in terms of mathematics, and make further progress with the problem as a result are valuable proficiencies, and ones which are widely applicable.

One useful perspective is to view modelling as a technique that is something of an art form. Pupils should be encouraged to model what they can within their own ability and knowledge, and then 'fill in' any gaps with discussion and justification. As pupils move through the school their models should then become more mathematically sophisticated and, in turn, more practically useful.

Mathematical models are used in many disciplines: for modelling whale populations for purposes of conservation; glucose induced insulin release in the human body; the compaction of rocks in sedimentary basins; and how pesticides spread through different types of soil. A recent paper (Munz *et al.* 2009) even modelled the effects of an outbreak of zombies, and came up with some suggestions on how best to deal with such a scenario! Models are used particularly widely in the fields of business studies and economics.

Examples of models from business studies and economics

A key topic in economics is the idea of supply and demand. In brief, this holds that in a free, competitive market, price and demand will influence each other and both will move to an economic equilibrium. This is well illustrated by a mathematical model of petrol price, adapted from Beare (1991: 6–12).

At the time of writing, petrol prices are very high, and it is not unusual to see prices of 120p per litre. Given the current climate, it would advantage an independent petrol station to lower their prices, but if their prices were to lower too far, say below a purchase price of 108p per litre, they would not make any profit. Mathematical modelling allows the owner to ask 'what if…?' without serious financial consequences; is it a low-risk first step to making a sensible business decision.

Let us say that at the current selling price, the petrol station is selling 20,000 litres per day. From experience, the owner of the petrol station suggests that dropping the price by one penny per litre would increase sales by 3,000 litres each day. This situation can be represented by the following equations:

$$\text{Quantity Sold} = 20{,}000 + 3{,}000 \times (\text{Original Price per litre} - \text{New Price per litre})$$
$$q = 20{,}000 + 3{,}000\,(120 - p)$$

$$\text{Revenue} = \text{Quantity} \times (\text{New Price per litre} - \text{Cost per litre})$$
$$r = q\,(p - 108)$$

If we substitute the top equation into the bottom, we get an expression for the revenue as a function of price:

$$r = (20\,000 + 3000(120{-}p))(p{-}108)$$
$$r = -3000p^2 + 704\,000p - 41040000$$

This describes an inverted parabola with a single maximum which can be found either through trial and improvement, the use of a spreadsheet or graphing package, or through differentiation. The optimum value of p, to the nearest penny, is 117p. However, the answer should not indicate the end of our interest with the model, as it is important to interrogate it and assess the validity of its findings: is this a sensible answer? Is the modelling assumption of a linear relationship between the drop in price and the increase in custom fair? Could we model the influence of the prices set by competing garages?

A similar concept in business studies is the 'break-even point', the point where the total costs of a business are equal to its total revenue. This concept is particularly important for start-up businesses, and it can be used to help assess the viability of a business plan.

As an example, consider a new business which plans to make and sell cushions. Items such as the machinery required give rise to fixed costs of £1,500. Each cushion costs £3 to make and is being sold at £5.99. To calculate the break-even point we must put total costs equal to total revenue. If we sell x cushions, this can be expressed by the equation:

$$1500 + 3x = 5.99x$$

This is a linear equation, and so we can solve it without recourse to a spreadsheet, and find that the company must sell 502 cushions before making a profit (they might want to raise their prices!) Although it is not necessary mathematically, it can also be useful for a pupil's understanding of the finances to draw a graph of this situation; the lines of cost and revenue are simultaneous equations, intersecting at the break-even point (Figure 7.4).

It is important that the pupils recognise that whilst the break-even point is a useful précis of the situation, it has been derived from a mathematical abstraction. Is it practical to make 502 cushions, or do cushions need to be made in batches of 10? Are the costs of making each cushion truly independent of quantity, or will it become cheaper to make the cushions after a certain point? Are all cushions sold at £5.99, or is there some variation

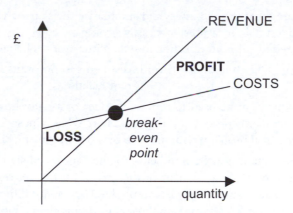

Figure 7.4 The break-even point as the solution of simultaneous equations.

in the price? Evaluation is a key part of the modelling process; in this case pupils might wish to informally recognise the potential for error, and expect instead to break even somewhere between 450 and 550 cushions.

These two models are offered as simple examples which could be utilised in the mathematics classroom; however, they barely begin to illustrate the range and complexity of models that are used in business situations. In retail, for example, mathematical models based around probability are used to determine the quantities of stock that should be ordered to maximise profit; in finance models are used to calculate optimal rates of compound interest; and in manufacturing linear programming algorithms, similar to those taught in decision and discrete mathematics courses, are used to deduce how resources should be used to generate the largest profit. These models range from the simple to the complex, but they can be immensely important and widely recognised; the 1997 Nobel Prize in Economics was awarded to two economists, Robert Merton and Myron Scholes who, together with Fischer Black developed a model that described financial markets and derivative investment instruments.

Modelling is a key part of mathematical literacy, and a skill which has relevance in many areas of the secondary curriculum. It is important, therefore, to provide pupils with a range of contexts within which to practice modelling, in order to enable them to be able to apply mathematics independently in the unknown contexts of the future.

Modelling also offers pupils an opportunity to develop their communication skills, as pupils are forced to justify their assumptions and answers. In addition, detailed modelling in the classroom can require pupils to work collaboratively, just as it does in real business environments. Different members of the team bring different skills, knowledge and understandings that all influence the construction and refinement of the mathematical model.

Mathematics in business studies and economics

Whilst mathematical models play a key part in business studies and economics, these two subjects contain a number of other mathematical elements which also offer opportunities for cross-curricular links. Four of these are offered here as examples:

■ Ratios are often used to assess and summarise the state of a business. For instance, the acid test ratio measures how easily a company could pay off its current liabilities if required to, without resorting to selling inventory. The ratio is given by:

$$\frac{\text{Cash} + \text{Short-Term Investments} + \text{Accounts Receivable}}{\text{Current Liabilities}}$$

This context can be used to explore the idea of a ratio: how does this qualify as a ratio, since it only produces a single number? What values would alert you that there was a potential problem with the flow of money in the business?

■ Businesses often utilise a number of mathematical and statistical tools to help with their decision making. As part of their work on market research, pupils studying GCSE business studies may be required to learn about different forms of sampling, such as random and quota sampling, considering demographic characteristics such as age, gender and socio-economic group. Similarly, when studying the processes of production, students are likely to come across topics such as critical path analysis, and statistical measures in quality control.

■ Economics can serve as a useful alternative context for teaching some of the principles of calculus. For example, the second derivative is traditionally connected with the idea of acceleration in the field of mechanics; however, it can also be contextualised in the field of economics, since the second derivative of a price index reports the rate of change of inflation. This is an important statistic as it reflects the health and direction of the economy.

■ Economics contains a number of other key measures, including the Price Elasticity of Demand. This is a ratio that reports the percentage change that might be expected in the demand for a service or product if the price was to change by 1 per cent; in this way it is connected to the petrol station model discussed above. The PED is calculated by dividing the percentage change in the quantity demanded by the percentage change in price. Whilst measures such as these are sometimes introduced qualitatively at GCSE level economics, a quantitative approach can help pupils to develop a finer appreciation of the concept. For example, why is the value of the PED usually negative? If we were to draw a graph of price against quantity, what would a totally inelastic demand (PED = 0) look like? What would a totally elastic demand (PED = infinity) look like? What about a unit elastic demand (PED = -1)?

Many of the links between mathematics, business studies and economics also have wider applications; there are a number of discrete qualifications available in the area of finance, and some of the diploma qualifications contain aspects of finance and business planning. There is also a lot of potential for using ideas from business studies and economics in cross-curricular activities that stretch across multiple subject areas. For example, you might calculate the payback periods of various energy efficiency technologies, or link to citizenship by seeing how different groups of people would benefit or suffer after a budget.

Summary

The National Curriculum for mathematics holds that 'mathematics equips pupils with uniquely powerful ways to describe, analyse and change the world' (QCA 2007: 139).

However, if pupils are to be properly equipped to do this, they need to be aware of the power of mathematics and have experience of using it in a variety of ways.

This requires them to work in a range of contexts, developing their capacities to use and critique algorithms and processes, and also to model real-life situations mathematically. This can happen in all subjects, but curriculum areas such as ICT, business studies and economics are particularly amenable to such work, as they contain elements and ideas that pupils can either manipulate directly, or connect to their own real-life experiences with money.

Mathematics is sometimes held to be a subject that deals exclusively in absolutes, making definite and unequivocal predictions. However, applied mathematics does not always operate in such a straightforward way. When pupils experience mathematical modelling first-hand they can move away from rigid preconceptions of 'right or wrong' answers and recognise the place of opinion, prediction, trial and improvement and realistic assumption. This understanding is an important facet of mathematical literacy, and a necessary one if pupils are to sensibly interpret the simplified mathematics and statistics that are reported by the media.

Professional Standards for QTS

This chapter will help you meet the following Q standards: Q8, Q10, Q14, Q17, Q23.

Professional Standards for Teachers

This chapter will help you meet the following core standards: C8, C10, C15, C17, C27.

Further reading

English, C. (1999) 'Modelling for the New Millennium' in Hoyles, C., Morgan, C. and Woodhouse, G. (eds) *Rethinking the Mathematics Curriculum*.

This chapter argues that modelling is an increasingly important skill in modern society, and offers a number of examples of mathematical modelling that you might like to adapt for your own classroom.

8

Pattern and pedagogy: mathematics and dance, drama and music

Out of all the subjects contained in the secondary National Curriculum, the performing arts subjects are perhaps considered to be the furthest removed from mathematics in both tone and content. This understanding has no doubt grown out of the stereotypical ways in which these subjects are often presented: mathematics as purely abstract, academic and acultural, and the performing arts as physically expressive, largely emotional and built around entertainment.

The idea of a strict dichotomy is fallacious, as many of the fundamental ideas of mathematics are present throughout the performing arts. Notions such as sequence, structure, pattern, symmetry and even ratio all play a significant role in the creation and performance of dance, drama and music, and many of these functions can be explored productively in the secondary mathematics classroom.

However, a cross-curricular approach to the performing arts can consist of much more than simply recognising these associations and offering occasional examples. The performing arts are often taught and delivered by teachers using pedagogic approaches and ideas that are vastly different from those typically used in the mathematics classroom. Many of these methods have the potential to be adapted for the teaching of mathematics, helping mathematics teachers to inspire pupils to explore and learn about the subject in a fresh and often highly motivating way.

Each section of this chapter will begin by looking at some of the specific links that exist between mathematics and each of dance, drama and music. It will then go on to consider how the mathematics teacher might benefit from adopting pedagogic techniques and principles drawn from these performing arts. As part of this, it will also describe a number of activities that you might like to try yourself.

Key objectives

By the end of this chapter, you will have:

■ Explored some of the links between the subjects of mathematics and dance, drama and music

- Considered how a cross-curricular approach can involve shared elements of pedagogy as well as shared content
- Evaluated some of the theoretical ideas which support the use of performing arts approaches in the mathematics classroom
- Critically considered the potential benefits and pitfalls of using such activities in your own classroom

Mathematics and dance

A number of mathematical ideas lie beneath both the aesthetics and the performance of any dance. One of the most obvious of these is symmetry. Line symmetry is present in many moves and positions used by individual dancers, and rotational symmetry is present in a number of traditional dance forms, such as maypole dancing and barn dancing. More abstractly, it is also possible to think of some dance moves in terms of symmetry through time; a move performed and then reversed could be understood to be temporally symmetric. It has even been suggested (Brown *et al*. 2005) that the degree of bodily symmetry a person possesses is associated with how well they dance.

Watson (2004) identifies four elements common to both mathematics and dance: spatial exploration, rhythm, structure and symbolisation. A consideration of these elements can lead to some interesting cross-curricular tasks. Tytherleigh and Watson (1987) describe one such activity based around a morris dance, where groups of four pupils were given the task of continuing a traditional dance for 24 counts. Each group was given the constraint that its members had to finish in the same position that they had started. This served as a significant constraint which forced pupils to recognise the need for inverse movements.

Another activity could be based around positioning a corps de ballet on a stage. This is the group of dancers in a ballet that forms a unified, moving backdrop for the soloists. The way that the corps de ballet is positioned often involves symmetry, rows, columns and even triangular formations. How many ways could the pupils arrange ten such dancers on stage so that the arrangement was symmetrical?

The need for dances to be written down and communicated gives rise to a real challenge: could the pupils devise a system of symbols for notating movement? There are a number of different ways to approach this problem, and pupils studying dance at an advanced level may have already come across systems such as Benesh Movement Notation, and the mathematically flavoured Laban Movement Analysis.

Whilst contexts and ideas such as these are undeniably interesting, it can be challenging to integrate them practically into the mathematics classroom on a regular basis. In such instances it is worth thinking about collaborative working. If you consider using the ideas in this chapter you may want to work with colleagues from the performing arts, if only so that you can use the spaces and facilities that they have at their disposal.

The value of dance to the mathematics teacher stretches far beyond shared contexts. The working definition of 'cross-curricular' presented in Chapter 1 started with the idea of 'knowledge, skills and understandings from various subject areas.' However, it then moved on to stress that these should 'inform an enriched pedagogy which promotes an approach to learning which embraces and explores this wider sensitivity through various methods.' (Savage 2011: 8–9) Cross-curricular teaching, therefore, is not just about shared content, but also about shared pedagogy. It is perhaps in this sense that the performing arts can impact most fully on the teaching and learning of mathematics.

Mathematics and movement

The usually static nature of the mathematics classroom can sometimes blind us to the fact that much of mathematics grows out of the perception and abstraction of actions (Piaget 1970: 16–17). In number, the symbols that we use represent abstractions of the physical action of counting, and much of geometry arises from the modelling and representation of movement. By making mathematics static we lose much of its richness; ideas drawn from dance can help make mathematics teaching more dynamic.

For instance, consider the first element identified above by Watson (2004), spatial exploration, or the study and representation of three-dimensional space through bodily movement. Transposing the idea of spatial exploration from dance into the mathematics classroom gives rise to a number of practical activities. At the simplest level, a pupil might spin around to trace a circle with their hand, implicitly and informally establishing it as the locus of all points equidistant from a fixed point. Watson (op. cit.) describes an activity where pupils explore the geometric properties of a cube by imagining they are inside it, then being instructed to touch vertices, midpoints and faces. This idea could be extended to other three-dimensional shapes to develop pupils' ability to think geometrically. For instance, such mental exercises can be used to introduce the idea of a dual polyhedron, the shape created by interchanging the faces and vertices of another polyhedron. Imagine that you are inside a cube. Place a mark at the centre of each of the faces, and join the marks up with lines. What new polyhedron have you created? What would have happened if we had started with a tetrahedron?

Although these ideas at first sight might seem unusual, or even frivolous, they can be incredibly motivating for pupils. Furthermore there are a number of theoretical models which strongly support the use of physical action as part of pupils' learning. One of the most prominent of these was outlined by the cognitive psychologist Jerome Bruner. Bruner proposed that there are three modes of representation: enactive, iconic and symbolic. Whilst these are not strictly hierarchical, they do represent sequential levels of sophistication, as learners move from actions to images, and then to language and other symbolic systems (Bruner 1966). The first enactive stage is an important one, and it can be beneficial to introduce even advanced mathematical concepts such as calculus in an enactive, or a combined enactive and iconic way, by getting pupils to visualise local tangents and slopes through moving their hands along the path of curves. Once this basic enactive understanding has been established it can be used as a foundation for more formal modes of understanding.

A number of similar 'enactive' activities can be constructed around the themes of co-ordinates and graphs. You might choose to arrange the pupils in a grid (perhaps using a paved area in school or the approximate grid provided by having desks in rows) so that the position of each pupil can be described by a Cartesian co-ordinate. By asking pupils to put their hand up if their y-value is twice their x-value, the teacher can demonstrate that y = 2x is a straight line graph; this method can also be used to highlight subtler points, such as the oft-neglected fact that the line y = 0 is equivalent to the x-axis. Polar co-ordinates can also be explored using through action; to this end the children's game

'Marco Polo' can be re-imagined as 'Marco Polar'. Begin by blindfolding one pupil in the centre of the room, and explain to them that they are standing on the pole, with the polar axis reaching out directly to their right. When they say 'Marco', another pupil has to say 'Polar'; the first pupil then has to describe the second pupil's position using polar co-ordinates. Through doing this the pupils develop their sense of the polar co-ordinate system and become more familiar with the components of polar notation.

Similarly, it can be productive to get pupils to create a 'human' bar chart by placing themselves physically in a category. This kind of approach can also be helpful when teaching scatter graphs; as pupils place themselves with respect to the two axes they come to realise that each point on a scatter graph represents one person, and grow to understand the nature of bivariate data. Although activities such as these are not cross-curricular in the sense of shared content, they do reflect a pedagogy that has been enriched by elements drawn from other subjects; in this case the idea of spatial exploration and mapping from dance.

It is worth noting at this stage that the idea of an enactive mode of representation resonates strongly with the principles of constructionism as described in Chapter 4. For instance, the 'total turtle trip theorem' can be adapted as an enactive activity. If the pupils walk around a path in the shape of a polygon, they will see that they have undergone one whole turn, and so recognise that the external angles of a polygon have to sum to 360 degrees. Here the pupil has replaced the 'turtle', constructing a physical path with their own movements and enacting a mathematical result.

A second theoretical model which can be used to support the use of physical activities in the classroom is the theory of multiple intelligences, developed by the developmental psychologist Howard Gardner. This model proposes that the idea of a single quantity known as 'intelligence' is flawed and over-simplistic, and that in fact humans can be intelligent in a number of different ways (Gardner 2006). The idea of multiple intelligences has been influential in supporting the promotion of 'learning styles' in schools, and at the time of writing, many schools actively encourage their pupils to label themselves as primarily 'visual', 'auditory' or 'kinaesthetic' learners. Likewise, teachers are encouraged to teach lessons that include elements that will appeal to all of these styles of learning.

Gardner's ideas, however, are controversial. The theory of multiple intelligences does not convincingly account for some features of general intelligence, such as processing speed, and is constructed in such a way that it is potentially unfalsifiable. Similarly, at the time of writing there is no empirical evidence base for the VAK model of learning styles, and many scientists have gone on record saying that the ideas behind it are 'nonsense', and this is not how the brain is known to work (for examples see Henry 2007). Nevertheless, it is fair to assume that pupils will be *motivated* to learn in different ways, and also that variety in planned activity can help to engage learners. In this way, it might be productive to use the VAK template as a prompt, rather than a prescriptive template.

So-called 'kinaesthetic' activities can also promote team work, in a similar manner to many of the activities that take place in dance. For instance, you might divide a class into two or three teams and then challenge the teams to physically form (or suggest the shape of) an isosceles triangle. The first team to successfully do so wins a point. You might then move onto more complicated shapes, such as a trapezium, a cylinder, or even challenge them to physically represent a more abstract concept such as positive correlation. To develop pupils' PLTS even further, you might introduce additional rules, such as not being allowed to communicate verbally. Once again, this kind of activity is not cross-curricular in the sense of shared content, but it does embrace the idea of shared pedagogy. As it resonates with some of the skills and activities that are used more commonly in dance and drama it is an opportunity to work in a truly cross-curricular way with teachers of those subjects, both meeting your objectives and those of the performing arts teacher.

Mathematics and drama

The subject of drama also involves elements which can be explored using mathematical ideas and tools. Drama is about telling stories, but in order to do this it relies heavily on sequence and structure, and both of these elements can be mapped and modelled graphically. An example of an analytical approach to structure can be found in the work of the dramatist Gustav Freytag. Freytag proposed that the action in Greek and Shakespearean drama followed a dramatic arc of five parts: exposition, rising action, climax, falling action and dénouement. This can be represented graphically, as shown in Figure 8.1.

Of course, not all dramas follow this pattern; many modern works follow a more complicated structure. Representing these new structures in a similar graphical way could help pupils explore and summarise the differences in structure between different works. Although these graphs focus largely on qualitative features, they can serve in the mathematics lesson as interesting additional examples of 'real-life' uses of graphs; they might even enable pupils to link the topic of graphs to an episode of a television show they had watched the previous evening! A similar activity could be based around using graphs to plot the rise and fall of different characters throughout a play. For instance, a pupil might be encouraged to sketch a summary graph using two different colours to represent how the families of Macbeth and Banquo grow in power and come undone throughout Shakespeare's *Macbeth*. Another important element of drama is sequence, and it would be suitable for students to structure and plan practical work in drama by using flow diagrams.

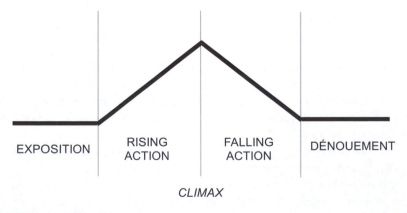

Figure 8.1 Freytag's Pyramid.

There are a number of other ways in which mathematics can be used in drama contexts: for instance, scale modelling is used when students are involved in set design, and costume design tasks usually require pupils to work to a budget. In a similar manner to dance, though, some of the examples described above are not ideally suited for the mathematics classroom. Once again it is valuable to focus on the pedagogic potential of using drama in the teaching and learning of mathematics.

Acting mathematically

One of the lessons which I personally used to dread teaching the most was introducing the names and properties of quadrilaterals. Although this lesson has a particular importance and place in the curriculum, I found that many pupils found the required content rather dry and uninspiring. In order to address this, I decided to introduce some drama. Pupils were challenged in groups to present a quadrilateral as if they were on a television shopping channel; this required them to focus on describing the shapes in great detail, outlining each of the properties as if it were a 'selling point'. Pupils' observational humour often complemented the mathematical classification: 'of course this shape has parallel sides, which we know are all the rage this season!' (Ward-Penny 2008).

This type of activity can be adapted for other topics, such as parts of the circle, or based around other programmes, such as television crime reports ('Have you seen this trapezium in your neighbourhood? Don't have nightmares…'). In each case, the use of drama can have a positive effect in a number of ways. From a mathematical point of view, it can focus the pupils' attention on the key skills involved: identifying geometric characteristics, then classifying shapes according to these features. In terms of classroom practice, it encourages pupils to participate in an active way, and appeals to the sensibilities of some pupils who might not otherwise be inclined to engage with the mathematics. The use of humour and the blending of content with performance can also make participation less threatening. Pupils are no longer assessed on whether they have completed an exercise in a single, correct way, but on a spectrum that reflects their wider understanding of the content. This is not to say that such activities should replace written or formal tasks, but they can certainly be used to complement them.

Another approach to using drama in the mathematics classroom is to encourage pupils to adopt the 'mantle of the expert' (Heathcote and Bolton 1995). This strategy is based around the idea of pupils positioning themselves as experts in a given field. The pupils are presented with a problem, often by a teacher acting as a client, and they then have to proceed with this enterprise.

For instance, the teacher might approach the pupils as the owner of a new casino, asking them to devise a game which would appeal to customers but favour the house in the long run. Each group of pupils would then have to design a game, calculate the appropriate probabilities, and finally report back to the casino owner in a clear and convincing manner. Alternatively, the teacher might be a council worker, who gives the pupils blueprints of an old building, and asks them to work out how to add ramps and other features to allow disabled persons to access the building in line with current legal regulations and requirements. Then again, the teacher might represent a cable television company, who asks the mathematicians to find the cheapest way to connect a network of ten towns. In each case, through taking up the mantle of being mathematicians, the

117

pupils are encouraged to work from a specific point of view, adopting patterns of behaviour and language that they see as being appropriate for mathematics.

The 'mantle of the expert' approach can be extended further, by asking pupils to imagine themselves as historical mathematicians. They might even be asked to solve genuine historical problems, such as how mathematicians originally calculated the height of the Great Pyramid, or estimated the circumference of the earth; such historical approaches often only used secondary school level mathematics. Ultimately, by insisting that pupils act in the role of mathematicians, they perform the work of mathematicians, utilising techniques and approaches in an authentic way and moving towards a fuller understanding of the power and relevance of mathematics.

Performing mathematics

Before moving on to discuss music it is valuable to recognise that mathematics is also present in some of the more unusual performing arts. For instance, the circus art of juggling contains a substantial amount of mathematics (Polster 2003). Juggling patterns can be represented with juggling diagrams. These diagrams display the vertical displacement of balls against time, with each 'beat' being represented by a circle; solid circles represent both odd beats and movements of the left hand, whilst open circles represent even beats and indicate catches and throws made by the right hand. The numbers underneath the diagram indicate for how long each ball is in the air. For example, Figure 8.2 shows two balls being juggled in the left hand, with each ball staying in the air for four counts at a time. Figure 8.3 represents three balls being juggled by both hands in a cascade.

Polster (op. cit.) goes on to provide some interesting questions: why would the juggling patterns given by 4, 4, 1 and 4, 1, 4 be equivalent? Why would a juggling sequence which contained the consecutive terms of *n* and *n-1* lead to a collision, and hence be unjugglable? Both of these questions can be answered by considering the shape of the associated juggling diagrams. Juggling mathematics also contains some results that would

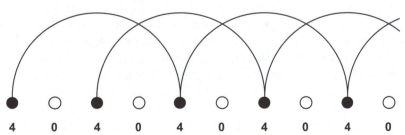

Figure 8.2 Juggling two balls with the left hand.

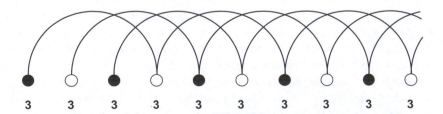

Figure 8.3 Juggling a three-ball cascade with both hands.

be easily accessible to pupils, such as the 'average theorem'. This states that the number of balls necessary to juggle a juggling sequence is equal to the average of the numbers used to represent the sequence (so the pattern 4, 4, 1 would require 3 balls). If you have an expert juggler amongst your pupils, you might even be able to enrol them as your assistant when presenting this context!

The discussion above has demonstrated that a very strong argument can be made for introducing subjects such as dance and drama into the mathematics classroom. However, it is often the case that teachers are not entirely comfortable using ideas and techniques from the performing arts in mathematics, and the majority of the existing practice in this area takes place with primary-age pupils. This issue will be explored further in Chapter 9, but it is worth taking some time at this point to consider your own practice.

Reflective task

To what extent do you feel you use movement and performance in your own mathematics teaching?

If you have used these types of activity in the past, do you feel they have been successful in promoting mathematical learning? How do you know?

If you have tended not to use these types of activity, what factors do you think might have prevented you from trying these sorts of approaches?

CASE STUDY: The Maths Circus

Nick McIvor is a mathematics AST based in London who frequently utilises performing arts techniques and pedagogy in his teaching and learning. Together with actor and science educator David Hall he has also combined a number of these activities to create a 'Maths Circus', a set of activities which motivate pupils to develop their number skills in a fun and unusual way that also encourages physical activity and teamwork.

One such activity is 'Number Juggling'. In this activity pupils have to focus on a physical activity – mimed juggling – whilst reciting a particular multiplication table in time with their physical movements. In one activity pupils start with one ball, such as '3, 3, 3, 3…', and are then fed additional 'balls' by a partner, moving to '3, 6, 3, 6…', '3, 6, 9, 3, 6, 9…' and so on. As the pupils become more confident they can increase the complexity of the mime by varying the rhythm, throwing balls under the leg or working in pairs and passing balls between themselves. Pupils might also be challenged to swap the direction of juggling at different points, and begin to count backwards. The reasoning behind this activity is that the physical movement partially redirects the pupil's concentration, and forces the pupil to learn the recited facts in a more robust way; the performance aspect also motivates the pupil to strive for mastery over the numbers in order to include more complicated throws and construct a winning performance.

'Galloping Gazintas' is another game which is designed to promote rapid recall of number facts. To begin with, each pupil is given an imaginary 'gazinta' with a particular number attached to it. The pupils then line up against one side of the room and, riding their 'gazintas', begin to gallop towards a marked out region on the other side. As they reach the half-way point the teacher holds up a larger number. If the pupils believe their number 'goes-into' the larger number, they enter the region; otherwise they turn back and return to the start. Here the inclusion of the performance aspect is designed to force recognition, rather than strict calculation. One enhancement of the game involves laying out two overlapping regions with different target values; the pupils then have to decide whether to enter one region, the intersection of both regions or turn back. The results of this activity lead pupils to discover the prime numbers for themselves.

Although these activities focus on basic number skills, Nick has also used a number of approaches that can work to illustrate ideas and concepts from more advanced mathematics. For example, the illustration of the 'Gallant Gauss Steppers' can be used to motivate higher attainers. The class is divided into two halves, and each half is labelled using the terms of the same arithmetic sequence. One team is placed in ascending order, with the other team placed standing opposite them in descending order. They then 'pair up' in a choreographed way and are asked to observe what has happened, then consider how this approach could be used to generate the formula for the sum of an arithmetic series.

Advancing even further along the syllabus, Nick has also taught the ideas of group theory to secondary school pupils using Scottish dancing. After playing around with various routines, the pupils were asked to consider the reflections and rotations that they had just danced through, and to try and note them down. This led to the construction of a basic Cayley table – introducing a high-level pun along with the high-level mathematics!

Nick believes that whilst these activities are highly enjoyable for the pupils, they also serve to improve the pupils' mathematics as well:

"The Maths Circus is now a key part of the year 7 intervention programme at my own school and I have seen it build confidence and skill levels across the borough. The idea of getting children to chant their tables is hardly new, but this approach means the activities can be sustained for long enough to have a real impact on learning without boring the learners."

Mathematics and music

Out of all of the performing arts subjects, music is the one that is most traditionally associated with mathematics; many of the connections between the two subject areas have been known for centuries. Pythagoras is credited as being one of the first people to recognise the relationship between basic number ratios and consonant musical sounds; it is said that he struck upon the idea after hearing a blacksmith strike out different tones when he used hammers of different weights. Whilst this story is probably apocryphal, the results uncovered as a result of Pythagoras' insight can be used in the mathematics classroom.

Each musical note can be expressed as a frequency in hertz (Hz); this is the number of times that the associated sound wave vibrates every second. For example, the A below middle C has a frequency of 220Hz, and the A above middle C has a frequency of 440Hz. These two figures demonstrate Pythagoras' first finding: that the frequencies of two notes an octave apart will be in the ratio 2:1. This can be enacted practically by showing that if you halve the length of a string it will vibrate twice as fast. Other combinations of notes that form intervals which sound pleasing to the ear follow similar ratios: a major third (made up of the first and third notes of a major scale) has a ratio of 5:4 and a perfect fourth forms the ratio 4:3. As the interval of a perfect fifth falls in the ratio of 3:2, the E above A has a frequency of 330Hz. In this way, musical intervals can serve as an interesting context with which to introduce the idea of ratio. However, it should be recognised that some stated values of modern pitches can differ very slightly; for example, using the ratio of 5:4 to find the C below E gives 264Hz, whereas it is currently held to be 261.626Hz.

This difference can be explained historically. Although the Pythagorean tuning system persisted for hundreds of years, it has some flaws which become readily apparent when music is transposed or moved up or down into another key. This led to the introduction of a new system of tuning, equal temperament, which is based around the principle that any two adjacent notes should have frequencies in the same, fixed ratio. It is an interesting exercise in geometric progressions to try and establish what the ratio between two semitones is, given that there are twelve semitones in a scale, and that the ratio of two notes an octave apart has to remain fixed at 2:1. It is then possible to see how much of a difference the new system makes to the frequencies of each note. Musically, the new system led to musicians being able to play in each major and minor key without retuning their instrument, and this new capability was exploited in the eighteenth century by J.S. Bach in his famous work *The Well Tempered Clavier*.

A more obvious use of number in music comes from the way that rhythm is composed, notated and understood. Most music naturally falls into a periodic pattern of accented strong notes and notes that are less pronounced. These accents help the listener identify a rhythmic shape to the piece of music being played. This is often helpful if the music is for a purpose: for instance a tango has a two-beat pattern (strong-weak) whereas a waltz has a three-beat pattern (strong-weak-weak). Most popular music is based around collections of three or four beats.

Rhythmic patterns can also be used to represent and explore patterns of numbers. For example, if half of a class was to clap on every second beat, and the other half of the class was to clap on every third beat, the class would clap together on every sixth beat. This type of exercise can be adapted to audibly illustrate the idea of lowest common multiples.

Musical notation can also give rise to a number of straightforward mathematical challenges. A crotchet (written as ♩) is worth one count, and so four crotchets would fit into a four beat bar. A minim ♩ is worth two counts, a semibreve ○ four counts and a quaver (♪, or ♫ for a group of two) half a count. Given that whenever a note is written with a dot after it, its length is increased by 50 per cent, can you work out:

- how many ♪ would fit into a ♩?
- how many ♪ would fit into a 𝅝?
- how many ♩ would fit into a ♩.?
- how many ♪. would fit into a ♩.?

Problems can be made more challenging by introducing semiquavers ♬, worth half as much as a quaver, or the symbols for rests, which indicate how much time should pass in silence before the musician plays the next note.

A more advanced, but more authentic challenge would be to present the pupils with the piece of music shown in Figure 8.4 which has three beats in each bar. Could they fill in the missing bar lines after every group of three beats? If the extract given finished at the end of a complete bar, how many beats is each 𝄽 rest worth? Tasks such as these are not dissimilar to activities that pupils sometimes complete in music lessons, or in early level music theory exams.

Figure 8.4 Adding bar lines to music.

Of course, rhythm does not only depend on the number of beats in a bar – but how fast they are going! Different genres of music are typically performed at different speeds, or tempos. Onion *et al.* (2008) discusses an activity contained in the Bowland Maths materials, which are discussed further in the next chapter. In this particular activity, 'My Music', pupils are encouraged to use music that they like as a source of statistical data, measuring the tempos of different tracks and making inferences about the tempos typical to different genres. They can then move on to look at other variables, forming and testing hypotheses about the features of different musical genres. How might the length of a typical track vary between different genres of music? What effects might listening to different genres of music have on pupils' heart rates? This can in turn give insight into answering some questions about music: why do composers choose particular tempos? How do the different tempos of the movements in a symphony help to establish different moods? What's the best music to listen to whilst jogging?

There are a plethora of other connections between mathematics and music (see, for example, Fauvel *et al.* 2003). Mathematical ideas are evident in the structure of music: for instance, when composers take a motif and develop it they use techniques which have parallels to some of the ways that mathematicians transform shapes: the motif can be reflected to form an inversion, translated through a musical transposition, and stretched in one dimension through elongation. The structure of tonal patterns and the operations can be explored further through abstract algebra; the twelve semitones in an equal temperament scale can be considered to form an Abelian group. Since the early twentieth century these ideas have been taken up and developed by mathematicians and musicians alike, and composers such as Schoenberg, Berg and Webern all used mathematical concepts in their works. Mathematical sequences are also featured in some twentieth century music; for example the French composer Messaien made use of some prime numbers to create unpredictable and unusual rhythms.

Mathematics of note

Alongside these direct content links, it is worth recognising that music can also influence pedagogy in much the same way as dance and drama have been shown to. One example of this is the construction of songs to help pupils learn mathematical concepts, or memorise mathematical facts.

Music has been shown to have a particular effect on the brain (Levitin 2007). Whilst this is complex and not fully understood, it is fair to say that the rhythm and structure of music can help in the processes of memorising and retaining information. This effect is compounded when a listener is exposed repeatedly to the same piece of music. For instance, imagine that you had heard a new song on the radio three or four times over the course of a day. How many lyrics would you be able to remember from the song on the next day? It is likely that you would recall more words, and retain them for longer, than if you had just studied a less structured piece of printed text for an equivalent amount of time.

Teachers have traditionally used this fact in the mathematics classroom to teach times tables through repeated chanting. This type of activity is suggestive of some of the ideas of behaviourism, as discussed in Chapter 3; it can be argued that the experience of partaking in the song acts as a stimulus which leads to the response of chanting the correct words. Repeating the same songs many times strengthens the association and reinforces the stimulus-response mechanism.

The power of music can be used for more than just learning multiplication facts, and a wide range of songs is available commercially and online for teachers to use in the classroom. However, the quality of these is variable, and they can seem childish to secondary age pupils. Therefore you might opt to challenge pupils to create and record their own songs, located in a genre of their own choosing. Condensing a mathematical idea into the framework of a verse or chorus can be very testing, as the pupils are required to isolate the important features of the concept and present them in a clear and meaningful way. Not all pupils are eager musicians, so it can be useful to implement a great deal of structure for tasks of this type; for example, you could split the class into four groups where three groups have to write one verse each on either the mean, median or the mode, and the fourth group has to write a chorus that explains what an average is. Furthermore, you might choose to work collaboratively with colleagues from the music department.

Finally, it is worth taking advantage of the back catalogue of tried and tested songs designed with a more adult audience in mind. In particular, you might like to use some of the songs of the mathematician, singer-songwriter and satirist Tom Lehrer; *That's Mathematics*, for instance, is a much briefer (and much wittier) version of the argument in Chapter 2 of this book!

Sharing pedagogy, improving practice

The opening chapters of this book began to put forward the case that in many schools the curriculum has become overly compartmentalised, with content and skills being taught discretely and without explicit connections. This state of affairs can work to the detriment of the pupils; after all, in the majority of cases authentic adult activity is cross-curricular.

A similar argument can be made to critique the way that certain pedagogical strategies are limited to particular subjects or groups of subjects. Adult careers usually require a wide range of modes of expression and a comprehensive set of skills. For example, whilst a professional mathematician will spend some of his time working alone on a piece of mathematics, he will also be required to present his work at conferences in an engaging way, write this work up as a paper, and probably work together with others in research groups. These tasks require them to draw on skills of presentation, performance, academic writing and team work. Presenting mathematics in a pedagogically narrow way is therefore both unhelpful and disingenuous.

Pedagogy can be borrowed from or used jointly with each of the school subject areas: mathematics can make use of the tools of physical construction from technology, and the framework of 'point-evidence-explanation' used in English is a good model for constructing statistical reports. The performing arts subjects go on to offer a veritable feast of pedagogical strategies with which pupils can explore and express their understanding and appreciation of mathematics in a safe and motivating way. As such they are not peripheral to cross-curricular teaching and learning in mathematics; instead they form the basis of a set of approaches which can reach and motivate many learners in a unique and powerful way. It is worth reconsidering exactly what truth might be contained in the phrase 'improving pupils' performance in mathematics.'

Professional Standards for QTS

This chapter will help you meet the following Q standards: Q6, Q8, Q10, Q14.

Professional Standards for Teachers

This chapter will help you meet the following core standards: C6, C8, C10, C12, C15.

Further reading

Bloomfield, A. and Vertes, B. (2005) *People Maths: Hidden Depths*.
This book is packed with classroom-ready kinaesthetic activities that will require your pupils to become moving pieces of mathematics. Each task is designed so that it can form the basis for group discussion and mathematical exploration.

9

Putting it into practice: mathematics, modern foreign languages and PE

The chapters leading up to this point have hopefully convinced you of the potential value of cross-curricular teaching and learning in mathematics, and demonstrated a range of ways in which cross-curricular practice might be brought into the mathematics classroom. However, before concluding it is important to recognise that cross-curricular activities do not offer an instant panacea for teachers; for such activities to work effectively they need to be chosen well and implemented appropriately. Cross-curricular opportunities can function as elements of good practice, but they do not automatically constitute good practice in and of themselves.

There are also a number of practical and pedagogical concerns that are associated with cross-curricular teaching. Is the mathematics teacher expected to be an expert in all subjects? How can they resource authentic cross-curricular contexts and ideas? How should assessment be conducted for projects that contain skills and content from a number of subject areas? How might the inclusion of cross-curricular elements be justified when time is limited and the syllabus has to be covered?

This chapter begins to explore some of these general questions and offers some suggestions about how you might overcome some of the common difficulties associated with cross-curricular activities in mathematics. As well as looking at more general issues, such as the use of technology in cross-curricular practice, it will also consider some of the curriculum areas not yet discussed, such as the modern foreign language subjects and physical education.

Key objectives

By the end of this chapter, you will have:

- Considered some of the additional practical demands made by cross-curricular approaches to teaching and learning
- Investigated some of the links between mathematics and other subjects including modern foreign languages and physical education
- Reflected on your own view of the nature and purpose of teaching

- Appreciated how the use of technology can enhance many cross-curricular opportunities
- Thought about how cross-curricular planning and assessment might be designed and managed

Mathematics and modern foreign languages

One of the school subject areas that has not yet been discussed is modern foreign languages. At the time of writing there are over twenty different GCSE qualifications in different modern foreign languages, including Spanish, Welsh, Urdu and Panjabi. There are also a number of other languages qualifications available, including qualifications in classical languages, NVQ courses in business French and business German, and a diploma qualification in languages and international communication. In these latter qualifications, mathematics can help support the wider study of languages in a number of ways; for example, statistical tools can help pupils to find out how widely and where different languages are spoken across the globe.

Sometimes a direct examination of other languages can give some insight into both the mathematics and language itself. The word 'hexagon', for instance comes from the Greek 'hex' meaning 'six' and 'gonia' meaning 'angle' – it is literally a six angle shape. The French word for 'eighty' also has an interesting etymology. Instead of using a new word for eighty, French expresses this quantity as *quatre-vingts*, literally 'four twenties', and subsequent numbers such as eighty five (*quatre-vingt-cinq*) have a similar compound form. This vigesimal pattern is Celtic in origin, and has echoes in some older English speech patterns, such as 'four score and seven years ago'. Languages where numbers are written as pictorial characters can be of particular interest to the mathematics teacher, as the composition of the characters can hint at the quantity being described and the underlying place value structure. When different languages are used in mathematics, even in such a basic way, it can help pupils to recognise the diversity of cultures in their classroom, and it is worth remembering that EAL (English as an Additional Language) pupils can serve as a resource in activities of this type.

Teaching mathematics in a different language

A more substantial cross-curricular challenge is to deliver a mathematics lesson in a foreign language, either independently or with the support of a colleague from the languages department. This idea forms the basis of the Content Language and Integrated Learning (CLIL) model, which is growing in popularity across the European Union and beyond. For the language teacher, CLIL lessons provide learners with more contact with the target language without adding more teaching hours. For the subject specialist, CLIL lessons can offer pupils a chance to explore their subject with a different perspective, forcing them to focus on how they are using language and concentrate more fully on the tasks given to them. The diversity of experience involved can also serve to increase pupils' motivation and confidence in both mathematics and the foreign language.

Research seems to suggest that CLIL can have a positive effect on pupils' learning in mathematics. Jäppinen tested a large sample of Finnish school children who had been taught mathematics and science in three different languages: 60 per cent English, 30 per cent French and only 10 per cent Finnish. The test results of this experimental group tended to be equivalent to or higher than those of the control group who had been taught entirely in Finnish:

> According to the findings of this study, it seems that Finnish CLIL environments support thinking and content learning, in particular, in situations where the learner has to compare different concepts and meaning schemes with each other. This is assumed to be due to the analogical CLIL reasoning systems that are based on exactly the kinds of situations where the learner makes comparisons between two semantic systems of two languages and two or more underlying cultures. CLIL learners may get special practice in classifying concepts and meaning schemes, in noticing and creating links between concepts and meaning schemes, and in hypothesising diverse things.
>
> (Jäppinen 2005: 163)

The experiences described in this paragraph are resolutely cross-curricular, and offer a meaningful and reasoned approach to a skills-based curriculum. However, there are a number of current concerns and limitations. A fuller analysis of the results in the experiment described suggested that the more abstract concepts of mathematics had not been learnt as well by CLIL pupils. The CLIL approach might also not work equally well for all learners; Seikkula-Leino (2007) found that there were fewer 'overachievers' in CLIL mathematics classes. Interestingly, she also found that CLIL learners evaluated themselves as being weaker at learning foreign languages than pupils in non-CLIL classes.

Nevertheless, the idea of teaching mathematics in another language holds a lot of potential and interest, and bilingual education could become more prominent in the future. You might like to consider small-scale ways in which you could use of the CLIL ideas in your own practice, such as using an adapted activity or worksheet from a French textbook.

Expectations, knowledge and the cross-curricular teacher

The ideas and potential of CLIL are exciting, but they also have the potential to be intimidating. Speaking personally, I enjoyed studying languages at school and did relatively well. However, this was a number of years ago, and I would have to invest a significant amount of time and effort before I would be comfortable delivering even the most straightforward mathematics lesson in a language other than English.

This dilemma exemplifies one of the common barriers to cross-curricular practice. Moving beyond mathematics often requires the teacher to either master a great deal of new material, or to relinquish their standard position as the classroom expert. This is arguably one of the major reasons that cross-curricular practice tends to dry up as pupils get older and start to work in a more sophisticated way.

Fortunately, there are a number of practical strategies that can help resolve this problem. First, and perhaps most obviously, it is sensible to begin cross-curricular practice by playing to your own strengths. If you have been playing the clarinet for twenty years, it makes more sense for you to embark on a project that involves music rather than attempting to teach a lesson in Hebrew. Second, it is advisable to work collaboratively with colleagues to enable a range of cross-curricular opportunities. This not only means working jointly with colleagues from other departments, but also identifying skills that colleagues in the mathematics department possess and considering team-teaching or occasionally swapping classes. You may be able to get support from your local authority, or get help from a locally based Advanced Skills Teacher. Third, it is worth familiarising yourself with the wide range of available resources and training that can facilitate cross-curricular activity, and some of these are discussed below. Over time your own knowledge and experience will develop, and in this way a wider range of cross-curricular activity can become more comfortable and less intimidating. Finally, it is worth recognising that in many cases the pupils can themselves be a resource. Each pupil will have their own set of interests and capabilities, and some pupils might be willing and able to help you bring a novel context into the classroom.

Support from all of these quarters can help you manage the introduction of fresh material into the classroom. However, it is also helpful at this point to explicitly consider some of the different ways in which the role of the teacher can be understood.

Reflective task (Part 1)

Before reading any further, imagine that you had to explain the role of a teacher to someone who had never seen a school before. Briefly write down one or two sentences that you might use to describe what a teacher *is* and what a teacher *does*. Then put your suggestions to one side and read on.

Fox (1983) identified four different metaphors that are commonly used by people when they talk about teaching: transfer, shaping, travelling and growing. It is worthwhile considering each of these in turn.

- **Transfer** positions the teacher as a delivery agent, who has the task of conveying knowledge and information to the pupils, often through lectures and printed materials. The pupils themselves are containers, waiting to be filled, and trying not to leak.

- **Shaping** sees the teacher as a craftsman, moulding the pupils by providing them with a number of carefully selected experiences. These might include practical tasks or investigations where the teacher knows the outcome in advance and how the pupils should develop from the experience.

- **Travelling** understands the teacher as a guide and travelling companion, pushing the pupil on to complete learning journeys. These may involve open-ended exercises with unknown outcomes and elements of independent learning.

- **Growing** portrays the teacher as someone who cultivates and nurtures the development of their pupils. In some ways this is similar to the travelling metaphor, but activities are even less structured and pupils are strongly encouraged to reflect on their own growth and development.

Reflective task (Part 2)

Look back over your jottings from the first part of this task. What words did you use to describe the role of a teacher – in particular, what verbs did you use? Which of the above metaphors do you think best fits your understanding of the processes of teaching and learning?

It is possible to argue for and against each of these metaphors; your personal perspective will be something that depends on your own experiences of teaching and learning, as well as your wider philosophy of mathematics education (Ernest 1991). However, it is valuable to recognise at this point that each metaphor places a different set of demands on the teacher. For instance, the 'transfer' metaphor would seem to suggest that the cross-curricular teacher must have full mastery of any topic area that is invoked in the classroom; anything less would be likely to lead to a faulty or incomplete transfer of knowledge. On the other hand, the 'travelling' and 'growing' metaphors allow the teacher to discover new subject areas alongside the pupil; the teacher's role is now to steer their pupils' development in terms of skills and personal development rather than to cover an explicitly predetermined amount of content. The teacher is no longer required to be an expert in every subject area that might be encountered.

Of course, none of the metaphors entirely circumvent the planning process. It is always critical to think in advance about the timing of tasks, how you are going to assess pupils' efforts and attainment, and ways in which you can support pupils. For instance, if you are not well versed in a topic area, and are planning a substantial activity based around it, it is always worth having some books or website addresses to hand in the classroom so that you can research additional information if and when it is needed.

Finding resources and finding the time

Even when a mathematics teacher is well versed in another subject area, or is willing to incorporate something new from outside of mathematics, it can seem difficult to resource authentic cross-curricular activities. Whilst it can be very rewarding developing new resources from scratch, it can also be incredibly time consuming. Fortunately there are a number of ways to gain inspiration and gather resources that already exist.

First, it is worthwhile checking whether your department already has access to any cross-curricular resources. In particular, many of the newer textbook schemes are marketed as part of comprehensive programmes that include additional printed and ICT-based materials. Some of these incorporate cross-curricular activities, but they are sometimes hidden away in teacher packs and supporting digital media.

Other cross-curricular resources are available online. One outstanding example of this is the Bowland Case Studies (available free to schools in the United Kingdom at www.bowlandmaths.org.uk). These materials are based around problems that frequently use cross-curricular elements, and are aimed at pupils in Key Stage 3. Chapter 8 has already described the 'My Music' case study, and there are many others. 'Highway Link Design' requires pupils to plan and cost a village bypass, taking into account social, environmental and work-related concerns. 'Keeping the Pizza Hot' looks at the mathematics behind the science of cooling and asks pupils to consider what measures pizza delivery companies could take to ensure that pizzas are delivered whilst they are still hot. 'Product Wars' involves designing a new smoothie, using proportional reasoning to analyse nutritional content and geometric thinking to design packaging. There are over a dozen further case studies, and each is supported by a wide range of interactive resources and documentation.

Subject associations are also a very good source of ideas. The two largest associations for mathematics teachers in the United Kingdom are the Mathematical Association (MA) which publishes a number of journals including *Mathematics in School*, and the Association of Teachers of Mathematics (ATM) which publishes the journal *Mathematics Teaching*. Both of these journals contain articles which are pitched at secondary mathematics teachers, including many pieces with a cross-curricular flavour; a number of the references in this book refer to articles in these journals. Both of these associations also run conferences which give you the opportunity to meet other teachers and share good ideas. A third relevant journal is *Teaching Mathematics and its Applications*, published by Oxford University Press on behalf of the Institute of Mathematics and its Applications. This also contains a number of interesting articles but it should be noted that the content in this particular journal ranges from upper secondary to undergraduate level mathematics.

Finally, there is a fair range of websites and books that are packed full of ideas. Many of these have already been referenced in the 'further reading' sections of each chapter, but it is worth noting that there are an increasing number of 'popular' mathematics books available in bookshops. Books such as *Why do Buses Come in Threes?* (Eastaway and Wyndham 2005) are recommended as sources of good illustrations that show how mathematics is intimately connected to a range of everyday contexts.

Although cross-curricular activities can be time consuming to establish in the first instance, these resources can help address this burden. Furthermore, as with most lesson planning, once you (or someone in your department who is willing to share) have designed and delivered a lesson, the planning time is substantially reduced for the future.

Mathematics and physical education

Another school subject that has not yet been explicitly discussed is physical education, or PE. Many of the links between PE and mathematics are similar to those that exist between mathematics and dance; for instance, balance and gymnastic exercises are frequently concerned with the issues of shape and symmetry, whilst Olympic diving demonstrates the idea of rotation in three dimensions. Some sports also have a correspondence with topics typically studied in physics; the mathematics of projectiles tells any prospective shot putters that the optimum angle of throw is 45° to the horizontal.

PE based exercises can also serve as excellent sources of data. For example, you might take the pupils outside for a practical activity: ask them to measure their heart rate, run for three minutes and then measure their heart rates a second time. Their measurements could then be used to construct a back-to-back stem and leaf diagram. For a more extensive activity, you might ask the PE department to conduct and then share the results of a 'bleep test', a fitness test which is often used in schools. This test requires participants to continuously run between points that are 20 m apart, reaching their goal before a 'bleep' sounds on an audio CD. The test is typically made up of 21 levels, and the score attained is usually given as the highest completed level. If the whole school had undergone a bleep test, it would be possible to plot the results of each year group as parallel box-and-whisker diagrams, and to calculate appropriate summary statistics. Pupils might link this work to careers by calculating what percentage of pupils in each year group would pass various organisations' fitness tests: the British Army asks that males under 30 achieve level 10.2, and that females under 30 achieve level 8.2, whilst the Royal Marines insist on a minimum level of 11.0.

Another measure of fitness is known as 'VO_2 max', the highest rate at which a body can transport and use oxygen. The exact calculation of this requires exhaustive testing, but there are a number of ways that this can be estimated. Two methods for the estimation of VO_2 max are the Cooper test and the Uth-Sørensen-Overgaard-Pedersen estimation. The equations for these estimates are, respectively:

$$VO_2 \text{ max} = (\text{distance in metres run in 12 minutes} - 505) \div 45$$

$$VO_2 \text{ max} = (15 \times \text{Maximum Heart Rate}) \div (\text{Resting Heart Rate})$$

Again, it would be plausible to work with the PE department to have pupils work out these values for their own body. Which of the estimates do they think would be the most reliable, and why? What were the absolute and the percentage differences between the two estimates? How important is cardiovascular performance in different disciplines? Published data is also available so pupils can compare their individual performance against typical values for non-athletes and athletes of different disciplines.

Mathematics can also be used to examine the development of sporting records over time. For example, the pupils might start by plotting the times of the male 100 m Olympic records against the years that the records were set. Can they fit a line to the data, or perhaps a curve? This type of exercise also generates discussion about extrapolation and the idea of a limit; why might it be meaningless to extend a trend line indefinitely in this case? More immediately, how do the school records of different events compare to the Olympic records? Statistical research and analysis could also be performed to investigate what effects altitude and ambient temperature have on athletic performance, and you might discuss why some sports professionals have specific training regimes to prepare them for different climates.

Sporting equipment and regulations can also provide interesting contexts for the mathematics classroom. For example, the centre of mass of a javelin is not half-way along its length; A-level mechanics students might like to experiment to find out where it is, and then consider what advantage this gives the thrower. In boxing, there are strict rules about weight limits, and matches are normally arranged for fighters of particular weight classes. Pupils could practice working with decimals by looking at the weights of famous fighters and placing them in the correct weight class. Finally, you might ask the pupils to evaluate the merits of the various systems that they are using to rank and compare performance in different sports. Many of these are easily criticised; Eastaway and Wyndham (2005: 132) give the example of the Olympic system, where countries are ordered by how many gold medals they have. This led to a situation in 1996 where Britain (one gold, eight silvers) was placed behind Algeria (two golds, zero silvers). Is this fair? Should points be awarded for silver and bronze medals – and if so, how many?

Using technology in cross-curricular activity

The quantitative analysis of performance and activity in PE has become more feasible with the increased use of technology in PE. Wearable items of technology such as heart-rate monitors and pedometers are becoming progressively more common, and some schools are using video to capture and analyse pupils' performance.

Another type of technology that is becoming increasingly common is GPS (Global Positioning System) technology, which can track your position in three dimensions. One activity that takes advantage of this technology is based around orienteering. The pupils begin by plotting a route on a map which shows the contours of the landscape. They then draw a graph which predicts how their speed (or displacement) will change over time, taking the gradients and geographical features of the surrounding area into account. After completing the planned walk, they can then compare their predictions to an actual, real-time graph.

Whilst this particular technology may be beyond the budget of many schools at present, technology in general is getting cheaper and more prevalent. This technology can often enhance, or even form the basis of, cross-curricular projects: digital cameras can help integrate ideas from photography and art, and data logging equipment can instantly quantify experiments drawn from physics. You may be able to borrow these types of equipment from other departments. It is also worth noting here that at the time of writing, graphical calculators are evolving dramatically, and that some of the most recent releases can help pupils to gather and analyse data in an 'on the move' situation.

Although the use of ICT has a number of associated strengths and weaknesses (Johnston-Wilder and Pimm 2005; Oldknow and Taylor 2003), it can be a particularly useful tool in cross-curricular activity. The government agency Becta (2009: 2) suggested that ICT could support the learning of mathematics in six main ways:

- learning from feedback
- observing patterns
- seeing connections
- developing visual imagery
- exploring data
- 'teaching' the computer

and each of these can be particularly relevant when planning and carrying out cross-curricular activities. For example, Ransom reports on a project conducted between mathematics and physics, where pupils used a motion sensor attached to a graphical calculator to generate distance-time and speed-time graphs. In this project the pupils benefited from having the chance to explore data *in situ*, to see connections between different representations of data, and to get instant feedback from their experiments.

The portability and immediacy of this technology gave students ownership of their experiments and allowed them to engage in higher order thinking skills such as making predictions, analysing data and modelling data with equations. Teachers reported in their logbooks that data capture was quick and easy, therefore students had immediate access. This encouraged the students to be critical and allowed them to retake readings if they seemed dubious ... There were many opportunities for extension work for the high attaining pupils as the equipment was easy to set up and menus were easy to master. Students seemed to have become more interested in learning mathematics and science.

(Ransom 1999: 3–4)

Multimedia technology can also offer novel ways for pupils to present their ideas and findings. For instance, you might ask pupils to create a short video on a theme such as 'measurement and units', 'moments' or 'rotations'.

However, whenever technology is used it is important to check that it is being directed to support the objectives of the activity, and not dictate them. This can sometimes be problematic in cross-curricular projects, especially when one of the objectives can be to become familiar and experienced with the technology being used. In such cases the activities need to be planned and structured so that the included mathematical activity is sustained by the use of technology and not relegated.

Mathematics and other subjects

The chapters of this book have discussed most of the subjects that pupils will encounter at secondary school level in the United Kingdom. However, this has not been an exhaustive survey, and other subjects can offer much to the mathematics teacher. Psychology, for instance, can offer a number of fascinating ideas which can lead to pupils designing experiments, collecting primary data and testing hypotheses. Could your pupils design and carry out a test that measured perception, or memory?

There is also a plethora of less common subjects that have not been examined for reasons of space: how might mathematics link to GCSE catering? Is there any potential for cross-curricular activity between mathematics and the public services diploma? Furthermore, how might the mathematics teacher respond to new qualifications that are introduced after this book is published?

The thematic discussions in the preceding chapters have given rise to a number of questions which should help identify possible cross-curricular links:

- Is there any shared *content*?

- Does the other subject contain *contexts* that either use explicit mathematics or involve basic mathematical ideas?

- Are there instances where *skills* developed in mathematics are, or can be validly used in the other subject? Indeed, are there instances where *skills* developed in mathematics may be learned more easily or effectively through the other subject?

- Can the other subject inform *pedagogy* in the mathematics classroom?

These questions are not exhaustive; for instance, you might also establish a cross-curricular link by looking at how mathematics and another subject are both used by a third subject. However, these four questions can be a useful starting point when trying to connect mathematics to other school subjects, or areas of study that lie outside of the school curriculum.

> **Practical task**
>
> Each of the following four subjects is offered as a GCSE subject in some schools. Using the list of prompts above, or otherwise, try to suggest one or two ways in which you might make a cross-curricular link between mathematics and each of these subjects.
>
> ○ Astronomy
>
> ○ Hospitality
>
> ○ Law
>
> ○ Journalism

It is also worth noting once more that there is no restriction that insists that cross-curricular work has to only take place between two subjects; after all, a lot of authentic adult activity uses skills and ideas from a large number of school subject areas. For instance, a project based around designing a new game would most likely use the mathematical ideas of probability and chance alongside skills drawn from product design and graphics. However, a pupil might also choose to look into the history of games, or even the psychology of games; this could in turn lead to considering the issue of gambling from a citizenship perspective. They might also opt to use ICT in the construction of their game.

The case study below details a set of activities which use knowledge and skills from a number of subjects to explore the theme of 'fortification', whilst keeping mathematics central throughout. This study also provides another example of how technology can be integrated into cross-curricular activity in a meaningful and supportive way.

> **CASE STUDY: Mathematics in Historical Contexts**
>
> Peter Ransom is a mathematics teacher at the Mountbatten School, Romsey, who has developed and used a large number of cross-curricular activities over the last few years. One set of these activities, based around the theme of 'fortification', was originally designed for use in regular mathematics classes but has since evolved into a Saturday morning master class for Year 9 pupils.
>
> At the start of the master class the pupils are introduced to the French military engineer Vauban (1633–1707) who served as an adviser to Louis XIV; Peter appears in costume as Vauban so that students appreciate the clothes and textiles of the time. Vauban was famous for his ability to design fortifications and spot weaknesses in the defences of others. Each group of pupils is presented with copies of historical texts in French and plates showing examples of military fortifications. This enables them to get a sense of the geometry involved by looking at symmetries and regularities in the designs.

The pupils then move on to constructing their own pair of proportional dividers. These are made by cutting out two identical lengths of card. Each length is marked up so that it is accurately divided into sixty equal sections. Finally a paper fastener is put through the two lengths so that the card can pivot and form two similar isosceles triangles. The proportional dividers can be then used to interpret scale drawings, but the pivot must be correctly placed for each different scale that is used. This poses a practical problem for the pupils that requires them to divide up a quantity using a given ratio.

During the class the pupils are encouraged to rationalise some of the choices that Vauban made and understand how, in the real world, mathematical and geometrical factors have to be balanced with other practical concerns. For instance, in one of Vauban's designs the fortifications were built in the shape of a seven pointed star. The pupils are asked to calculate the length of this shape's perimeter, and compare this to the perimeter of the heptagon that joins the outer points. They then have to argue why Vauban chose the shape that he did, and recognise that a small percentage increase in perimeter can lead to a much improved capacity to defend.

The pupils also look at the paths of projectiles. Using hand-held TI-Nspire™ graphing calculators they experiment with transformations of the parabola $y = x^2$, seeing how the equation changes as they drag and stretch it, and spotting for themselves patterns in the algebra. This task ends up with the pupils being given a profile view of a town. Their challenge is to find a parabola that will launch from the origin and fire onto the ramparts.

Throughout all of the activities the emphasis is on drawing skills and understandings from multiple subject areas; for instance, pupils also have to consider the geographical features of where fortified towns were positioned, and understand the defensive values of various locations. Music contemporary to the period, such as that of the French composer Lully is also played throughout the day to consolidate the historical flavour of the proceedings.

Another set of activities that Peter has developed is based around the legendary 'Dambusters' raid of May 1943. Dressed in the uniform of an RAF Flight Sergeant he challenges the pupils to serve as one of the navigators in the Lancaster bombers, deducing the bearings and distances that made up the famous five stage journey. Later on the pupils have to work out how to angle the lights at each end of the bomber in order to make the beams cross exactly sixty feet below the plane; this requires them to use either constructions or trigonometry. Finally the pupils use mathematics to plot the course of the bombs themselves, and their calculations are tested using computer simulations.

A third set of activities is based around the mathematics of the Battle of Trafalgar (for details, see Ransom and Shiers 2010). In each case Peter believes that the pupils benefit significantly from applying their mathematical skills in authentic historical contexts:

"For me and my students mathematics comes alive by seeing the contexts in which it developed and was applied. I always include some creative work, mostly by having students make simple replicas that they can use to investigate problems. With the fortification work some groups even made a model of the mathematics area of school and fortified it in the style of Vauban to deter invaders from a local school!"

The final part of this chapter will look at two more prominent questions: how might cross-curricular activity be planned, and how might it be properly and usefully assessed?

Planning cross-curricular activity

Planning is central to any teaching of mathematics; however, it is neither simple nor straightforward. Proper planning requires teachers to consider and interpret information drawn from a wide range of fields, including their mathematical subject knowledge and their understanding of pedagogy (Jones and Edwards 2010). The challenge of planning is particularly pronounced in the case of cross-curricular activity, as teachers are required to juggle and structure knowledge and skills drawn from more than one subject, whilst simultaneously trying to ensure that activities and objectives are meaningful, authentic and related to curriculum requirements.

This last condition can be particularly challenging. We have already seen in Chapter 1 that whilst cross-curricular elements are loosely prescribed by the National Curriculum, they are rarely if ever described; this accounts in part for the wide range in cross-curricular provision that is currently seen in English secondary schools. In many ways, this lack of specification is an advantage, for if cross-curricular activity was to become a statutory requirement it would undoubtedly limit the freedom that teachers currently have to move between subjects in a variety of creative ways. However, in other ways the slight manner in which cross-curricular activity is presented can suggest to teachers that it is an optional extra, and in some schools you may find yourself having to plan so as to defend the inclusion of cross-curricular elements against the tyrannical goal of 'covering the curriculum'.

There are as many ways to plan as there are cross-curricular activities. However, for the purposes of this discussion it is worth isolating four different starting points for planning cross-curricular activity: starting with an objective; starting with a context or problem; starting with a theme; and starting with staffing.

Starting with an objective

In this model, planning begins with an objective or topic in the syllabus and searches for a cross-curricular activity that matches it. For example, if you started with the topic of 'writing and ordering decimals' you might choose to: time your pupils running 100 m then ask them to order the results; discuss with the pupils how the decimal point is written in different countries; or present pupils with the percentage values of the twelve most common compounds in the chemical composition of air and ask the pupils to order them. This approach to planning can tend to give rise to smaller, 'easy to use' cross-curricular contexts, and these can be added onto schemes of work and other planning documents in a straightforward manner. However, the nature of the cross-curricular activity generated is often rather limited, and tasks usually require a very narrow range of skills. It can also be difficult to attach authentic contexts to some topics, such as 'dividing fractions'.

Starting with a context or problem

In this case, pupils start with a situation that is based firmly in real life. For instance, pupils might be asked to investigate whether renewable energy is going to be able to replace fossil-fuel-based power sources in the near future, or to look at an existing system used for making appointments in a doctor's surgery and suggest ways to make it more efficient. This approach to planning can lead to longer, more involved tasks which can take up entire lessons or sequences of lessons. These tasks can be highly structured, but tend to be more flexible than objective-led activities. As such they have the potential to be more authentic, and pupils can often use a wider range of skills; pupils are often more motivated if they feel they can make genuine choices and take ownership of the task. However, as the tasks become more genuine and open-ended, there is a risk that pupils might focus on aspects of the task that are not substantially mathematical. The diversity of possible responses can also make assessment difficult.

Starting with a theme

This model is often used in primary schools. Pupils are introduced to a theme which is then explored in many different ways across different subjects. For example, the theme of 'reflection' could be explored in mathematics whilst at the same time the pupils are studying the myth of Medusa in drama, the laws of optics in physics and the idea of meditation in RE. This model can be easy to manage, as departments are generally working independently. However, whilst it can be interesting for pupils to see how the same idea can be interpreted in a number of different ways, the resultant activities are often only superficially cross-curricular; in most cases there is no real shift in learning or pedagogy as a result of the theme.

Starting with staffing

This last model uses practical issues as a starting point. For instance, you might conduct a skills audit in your department and discover what extra-mathematical talents and interests your colleagues have. These could then be developed and extended into avenues of cross-curricular activity. This approach to planning is designed to encourage teachers to deliver material that they are comfortable with, and can be a non-threatening way to introduce cross-curricular elements. However, coverage can be erratic, and pupils may miss out on a number of exciting opportunities if teachers are only willing to link mathematics with science. It can also be problematic when teachers feel pressured to 'choose' a cross-curricular area. Similar problems can emerge at the level of the department; for instance, the school leadership might group together the subjects of maths, history, food technology and PE and ask them to produce a cross-curricular project.

Each model of planning has a different set of advantages and disadvantages, and in reality cross-curricular provision usually consists of a mixture of such approaches. However, the four caricatures above can serve as reminders of some of the issues that need to be held in tension: keeping contexts both realistic and manageable; drawing on other subjects whilst still delivering the mathematics curriculum; being confident in delivering material but still challenging yourself and offering a range of experiences to pupils; planning for differentiation but doing so with a view to managing assessment. There is no single correct model of planning that will address all of these issues, as each teacher is unique, and each school situation is different. Chapter 10 will go on to discuss how you might make some initial decisions in this respect.

Assessing cross-curricular learning

Assessment is one of the most problematic elements of planning for the cross-curricular practitioner. Whilst shorter in-class contexts generally fall in line with a teacher's usual assessment strategies, extended tasks can be very problematic. For example, suppose that pupils had been tasked with producing a video of a sketch that showed them using mathematics in a historical content. In this situation, there are many ways in which pupils can successfully use their skills and knowledge. They might have used editing software to ensure high production values, or endeavoured to use historically accurate language in their script. Their acting could be particularly convincing, or they might have explained some sophisticated mathematical idea through the words and actions of their characters. Which of these achievements should be considered the most important? Would it be possible to watch five such videos and give each a mark in a valid and reliable way? How should pupils' work be assessed when it involves skills and knowledge drawn from a range of disciplines?

Once again, there is no single, straightforward solution to this problem: ultimately it is a matter of opinion which rests on individuals' views about the purpose and nature of education. However, some practical steps towards a solution can be found within the ideas of Assessment for Learning (Black *et al.* 2003).

First, formative assessment sidesteps many of the philosophical problems inherent in summative assessment, as the focus is no longer on comparing pupils' work and declaring its value, but instead on developing each pupil as an individual learner. Using the example of the task above, it would be easier and more straightforward to praise each video on its strengths and then give each group of pupils a point of constructive criticism for future development. On the other hand, the absence of a final 'grade' might make it difficult for such cross-curricular activity to feed into the recorded assessment and tracking systems of some schools; furthermore, if cross-curricular projects were never graded but 'regular' tasks were, the cross-curricular projects might be devalued in some pupils' (and staff members') opinions.

The case study in Chapter 3 demonstrated an alternative approach. At the start of each project the pupils were explicitly told the assessment criteria that they would be judged against. Returning again to the example above, it would be possible to have assessment criteria presented in four separate strands: drama, media, history and mathematics. This approach can structure the formative assessment process so that some summary of pupils' successes can be recorded, whilst each group of pupils is still given relevant feedback. It also begins to address the issue of differentiation, as teachers can introduce and phrase the assessment criteria in a way that demonstrates different levels of expectation.

Another way of structuring the feedback process is to integrate peer- and self-assessment. This strategy has been shown to engage pupils more fully in the formative assessment process: 'Pupil self assessment has as a consequence that they are more motivated and conscious in relation to their work. They are more responsible and their efforts are more long term and goal centred'(Black and Aitken 1996: 110). In this way peer- and self-assessment also continues to develop the PLTS that cross-curricular activity often involves. Peer assessment is particularly easy to structure when the project has been based around a problem; in these cases pupils can vote for what they feel is the most successful or convincing solution to the problem. In many ways this approach reflects real world assessment exercises more accurately than any summative 'marks out of ten' model.

As was the case with planning, there is no 'correct' model for assessment; different approaches will have different levels of success depending on the structure and nature of the activities being undertaken. Furthermore, pupils who are unused to formative assessment techniques may need time to get used to them. In particular, the quality of pupils' peer-assessment will develop over time. However, it is critical to consider how you might choose to assess cross-curricular work before embarking on any extended activity or project in order to establish pupils' work as something worth valuing.

Summary

This chapter has explored some of the key issues associated with cross-curricular practice. However, in many ways it has raised more questions than answers. This is inevitable, as the arena of cross-curricular teaching and learning is vast and varied. Three colleagues might read this book and develop entirely different perspectives: one might be drawn to the idea of teaching mathematics through history; a second might be inspired by the examples of presenting mathematics through the performing arts; a third might dismiss both of these perspectives and instead focus on the use of more traditional science and technology contexts in the mathematics classroom. None of these perspectives is inherently superior to the others; however, all three should seek to engage with the questions raised in this chapter and develop their own answers in order to try and deliver the best cross-curricular teaching that they can. Perhaps the three perspectives will end up being complementary, and their pupils will benefit even further.

Of course, in many ways experience is better than theory, and your own practice will inevitably evolve and develop over time. However, if this is to happen effectively, it is important that regularly reflect on your current position, evaluate your methods, and then set yourself appropriate goals that will help you to move on in your cross-curricular practice. The final chapter of this book will offer some ways in which you might begin to do this, and help you to consider how you might find your own context for cross-curricular teaching and learning in mathematics.

Professional Standards for QTS

This chapter will help you meet the following Q standards: Q6, Q8, Q10, Q12, Q14, Q15, Q17, Q22.

Professional Standards for Teachers

This chapter will help you meet the following core standards: C6, C8, C10, C12, C15, C16, C17, C26.

Further reading

Bowland Maths: www.bowlandmaths.org.uk

The Bowland Maths case studies include a number of exciting, ready-to-use cross-curricular activities that are predominantly aimed at Key Stage 3 pupils.

In addition to these, the website features supporting professional development materials which address some of the concerns raised in this book about planning and managing cross-curricular activity. At the time of writing all of the materials can be accessed for free by UK schools.

10

Finding your own context for cross-curricular mathematics

This book began by stating its three interconnected aims: to justify the importance of a cross-curricular approach to teaching and learning mathematics, to provide a wide range of examples, and to explore both the potential and pitfalls of such an approach. Each of these aims has been addressed in a number of ways throughout the chapters of this book. However if these intentions are to have any meaning it is critical that you take time now to reflect on the preceding chapters and evaluate how they might impact on your practice as a mathematics teacher.

This final chapter is designed to help you begin this process of reflection and evaluation, and to guide you through some strategies for establishing personal goals that will challenge you to develop as a cross-curricular practitioner. Reflection is always a key element in developing practice, and it is particularly important in the case of cross-curricular activity. The vast range of possibilities and options that are available for working in a cross-curricular way, both in terms of content and approach, inevitably adds a personal element to cross-curricular practice. This range and diversity is a strength that can allow each teacher to engage with ideas and methods that suit them. However, reflection is necessary for you to be sure that as many avenues as possible are explored and for the available choices to become apparent.

Key objectives

By the end of this chapter, you will have:

- Reflected on your understanding of 'cross-curricular' teaching and learning, and considered how it might have already started to evolve

- Understood how cross-curricular approaches are influenced by choices and preferences at the levels of the teacher, pupils and school

- Challenged yourself to set targets and move forward as a cross-curricular teacher of mathematics

Choosing your own path

There is no single 'correct' way of approaching cross-curricular activity, and equally there are no 'right' answers to the questions of how best to plan, carry out and assess cross-curricular work. There is not even a universally agreed definition of what actually constitutes cross-curricular practice. This is somewhat inevitable; it is likely that even your own understanding has developed in some way as you have read through this book.

Reflective task

Chapter 1 offered the following working definition of 'cross-curricular' teaching:

> A cross-curricular approach to teaching is characterised by sensitivity towards, and a synthesis of, knowledge, skills and understandings from various subject areas. These inform an enriched pedagogy which promotes an approach to learning which embraces and explores this wider sensitivity through various methods.
>
> (Savage 2011: 8–9)

Has your understanding of this definition developed as a result of the discussions and examples of the previous chapters? Has your own view of mathematics and what constitutes mathematical activity changed over the course of this book? If you still have them available, you might find it insightful to compare your current thoughts with your jottings from the first reflective task in Chapter 1.

Cross-curricular practice also tends to be very diverse because it is subject to a wide range of personal and local concerns. For instance, when choosing a cross-curricular activity you will be influenced by each of the following perspectives:

Your perspective:

- What contexts and subject areas do you feel confident talking about?
- What areas inspire, interest or delight you personally?
- What types of activities do you enjoy using in your teaching?
- What do you think would challenge or develop you as a teacher?

Your pupils' perspectives:

- What contexts are current, relevant and interesting to your pupils?
- What sorts of activities do they enjoy participating in?

- What activities are rarely used as part of your pupils' learning so that they might find them new and exciting?
- What might be most appropriate for their development as mathematicians at this point?

Your school's perspective:

- What other subjects does your school offer which you might link with?
- Are there particular foci within the school that could provide a stimulus for the work, such as residential trips or fund raising events?
- What resources (such as technology, colleagues and alternative rooms) do you or could you have access to?
- How supportive would your managers and school leaders be if you wanted to try something that was very different to normal practice?

It is important to recognise that there are pressures associated with the answers of each of these questions. Sometimes you might come across conflicts of interest between different perspectives, or be limited in what you can comfortably do, or even in what you are permitted to do. Such issues can require a significant amount of thought. However, above all else these pressures and preferences should not be used as an excuse for giving up entirely, or failing to engage with the enormous potential of cross-curricular practice. Instead the answers to the questions given above should be used as a starting point with which you can begin to tailor and design your own practice.

Practical task

Flick back through this book and note down a handful of ideas that have interested you or appealed to you as a teacher. Now use the questions above to narrow this list down to two or three activities which you think would be most interesting to the pupils you are currently teaching, and which you could practically resource and deliver in your school.

Levels of cross-curricular activity

One way of beginning to audit or develop your own cross-curricular practice is to introduce the idea of four different levels of cross-curricular work. These levels are based loosely around the scale of the cross-curricular tasks being considered, and range from brief interjections and comments to extensive interdisciplinary projects.

The first level consists of *cross-curricular interjections*. These are comments, examples or illustrations which draw on ideas or knowledge from other subjects. For instance, when teaching percentages it can be useful to tell the pupils that the term 'per cent' is related to the French word 'cent' and the Latin word 'centum', which both mean one hundred. They might then be encouraged go on to make connections to other words used elsewhere in mathematics and in other subjects; why is the idea of 100 relevant to the meaning of 'centipede', 'centigrade', 'centimetre' and 'centenarian'? Similarly, when you are teaching the topic of shape, pupils might be interested to know that the French sometimes refer to mainland France as *l'hexagone* due to its shape. In many ways this category can be thought of as a cross-curricular general knowledge. This type of cross-curricular addition places a low level of demand on the teacher, and although individually such interjections are unlikely to have a huge impact on the learner, they can have a positive cumulative effect.

The second level is made up of *examples or short activities* which normally have a narrow focus and function as one part of an otherwise purely mathematical lesson. These are mainly used as illustrations of the mathematics, and so mathematical skills take precedence over other subjects. For instance, when teaching standard form you might present pupils with the volumes and masses of each of the planets in our solar system in standard form, and ask them to calculate the mean density of each planet. You might then ask them to use this information to speculate briefly on the variation in their results; for instance, gas giants will have lower mean densities. Whilst this level of activity can involve understandings and skills from outside of mathematics as well as imported knowledge, the focus tends to be firmly on the mathematical content. This type of activity requires some planning from the teacher, but the limited scope of the questions makes it easier to manage. Although the level of cross-curricular activity is limited, these contexts can have a very positive effect on pupils' motivation, particularly if they reflect a wide range of contexts which encompass the pupils' own interests; you might like to involve the pupils in generating and selecting contexts. This level could also be thought to include uses of pedagogy adapted from other subjects, such as the uses of poetry and language discussed in Chapter 5, or the use of kinaesthetic activities discussed in Chapter 8.

The third level is comprised of *extended activities with multiple sections*; these can take up a whole lesson, and explicitly use skills and understandings drawn from both subject areas as well as knowledge. As such, they often include questions or other elements which are not seen to be immediately mathematical. For instance, you might ask pupils to explore voting behaviour in the United Kingdom. There is a theory that good weather improves the chances of the Labour Party in English elections. Is the weather on the day of a general election correlated with voter turnout? Why might a higher level of voter turnout impact individual parties differently? The final question in this set relies predominantly on ideas and understandings drawn from politics; however, this is not to say that mathematical skills and ideas could not be utilised in order to answer it. This level of activity can require significantly more planning on the part of the teacher, as the issues involved can be explored in a variety of ways. However, the work produced is much more authentic in its scope, since pupils have to move between the artificial boundaries of school subjects. As they need to make more choices and decide how they are going to answer a question they are also more likely to develop as autonomous learners. It should be noted, though, that this level of activity is both rewarding and challenging, and that paradoxically some learners may need support to manage their freedom.

At the fourth level there are *interdisciplinary projects* which plainly stretch across subject areas and frequently use mixed approaches to pedagogy. For example, you might ask a class to compose a short piece of minimalist music that uses either the prime numbers or the Fibonacci numbers. Alternatively, you might challenge pupils to produce a five-minute news report on teenage pregnancy. Mathematically, this could involve analysing raw data to find statistical trends, comparing rates of teenage pregnancy across Europe, and presenting their findings graphically using ICT ready for inclusion in the report. It would also require them to consider social influences and relevant citizenship issues, then write and film their own news report using appropriate stylistic conventions. This level of cross-curricular activity is very demanding, and planning will often involve a number of colleagues drawn from different departments. It may also require an effort to synchronise schemes of work. Alternative curriculum structures, such as those discussed in Chapter 1 can make it much easier to manage such projects. Learners can benefit enormously from this kind of activity, in terms of both engagement and moving forward in their own development as learners. However, activities at level four need to be managed and integrated carefully into the curriculum to ensure that the content is meaningful and the benefits are channelled into pupils' wider study.

Before moving on, it is important to note that these categories are neither well-defined nor exhaustive. Some activities may be difficult to label, and it is almost always possible to extend or condense an activity so that it moves between levels. However, this model is a first-order approximation which can be used to set goals.

Setting goals for cross-curricular practice

Goal-setting is a personal process, and it is important that you choose your own targets and a timescale that you feel comfortable with. The ideas that follow in this section should be adapted to your own situation, and be tailored in light of your own experience.

Nevertheless, it is fair to argue that most teachers would choose to set goals that recognise the different levels of planning and involvement discussed above. For instance, you might set yourself the target of planning to use level one connections – brief interjections and asides that link mathematical ideas to other subjects – a few times each week. It is likely that you already do this, but conscious planning can help you audit and develop your practice in this regard.

Level two activities require a little more planning, and so you might set yourself the goal of using this sort of task at least once a week. Ideas for contexts and ready-made examples can be found in any of the resources discussed in the last chapter, or through an Internet search. As you continue integrating level two type activities into your practice it is worthwhile making a note of successful activities, and sharing them with your colleagues. You might also want to add some of these contexts and activities onto your department's scheme of work in order to save time and planning in the future.

Level three activities are much more ambitious. If you are an experienced cross-curricular practitioner, or if cross-curricular activity is a priority for your school, you might embrace this level of task readily. However, if you are starting out you might like to set yourself the target of using this sort of activity once a term, or even once a year. One approach is to identify areas outside of mathematics that particularly interest you and look for relevant topics. Another is to seek a like-minded colleague in another department. Equally, you might choose to use ready-made resources, such as the Bowland Maths materials. It is worth noting once again that these levels are not strict demarcations; as such, you might set yourself the goal of starting with level two activities and deliberately developing them over time to better integrate skills and understandings from other subjects.

Level four activities tend to be large-scale and demanding, usually requiring a number of colleagues to work together and dedicated curriculum time. Such tasks are a laudable goal, but you will need to set your own goal in light of your own school's resources and intentions with regard to cross-curricular practice.

In this way, the four-level framework can help you set goals. However, this does not constitute a comprehensive plan; it is also important to set goals that reflect upon the depth of content and thinking involved in each task. It is also worth thinking about different groups of pupils, to make sure you consider using cross-curricular contexts not only with Key Stage 3 pupils but with Key Stages 4 and 5 as well, or that you do not only use more ambitious activities with pupils that have been labelled as 'more able' through setting.

Practical task

This is the final task of this book, and you must now start to find your own context for cross-curricular mathematics by setting yourself some goals.

There are a number of ways to set goals and targets, but you might want to begin by considering these questions:

- What am I going to try? What am I going to try *first*?
- What do I want to achieve by using cross-curricular mathematics?
- When am I planning to try these things? With which groups of pupils?
- What support or resources will I need before I can begin?
- How will I know whether I have succeeded?

This last question is particularly important; it is inevitable that some activities will seem to work better than others, and you will need to consider mechanisms for feedback and evaluation which should then feed into future planning.

Before reading any further, take some time to note down in writing how you feel you might inform your practice as a result of reading this book. You might find it useful to look back at your notes from previous tasks, or to look over the lists of questions and planning suggestions that have been made in this chapter. There is no 'right' answer to this task, and it is important to be honest to yourself, recognising what interests you, what you feel confident doing and how the ideas raised in this book have challenged you.

Conclusion

In 1937 the American publication *National Mathematics Magazine* ran an article which proposed that it was time for a change in the teaching of mathematics:

> Frankly we must adjust our courses honestly to meet the present social conditions. A great deal of the content of our courses now taught more or less as an end in itself

must be offered as a means. The emphasis must be placed not so much on the abstract, and we must teach with both hindsight and foresight. To do this we must vitalize our mathematics … This demands of the college teacher a sympathetic attitude towards fields other than his specialty, and an earnest effort on his part to humanize his special field by relating it wherever possible to the kindred fields and to practical life and experience.

(Edington 1937: 28–29)

Edington's article makes a stirring argument for the recognition and promotion of mathematics as a discipline which is a vital part of society, underpinning and underlining other disciplines in a uniquely powerful way. Over seventy years later this call is ever more relevant; technological developments have enabled mathematics to be placed firmly at the heart of many traditional disciplines, and new disciplines such as computer science, operations research, game theory and bioinformatics continue to add to the abundance of fields that can be labelled 'applied mathematics'. The rapid speed at which society is developing, and the way in which the economy is depending increasingly on technologically skilled labour both suggest that the relevance of mathematics and mathematical thinking will continue to increase. Unfortunately this fact is not recognised in many mathematics classrooms. All too often pupils consider the purpose of a mathematics lesson to be getting full marks, or worse, simply marking time until the end of the hour.

Mathematics should be enjoyed, not endured. Cross-curricular activity has the potential to reclaim mathematics as a vibrant and vital subject, and to motivate its wider study. Using contexts from other STEM subject areas can help teachers and pupils celebrate the fantastic range of ways in which mathematics supports modern life, from making toast in the morning to sending satellites into space. Linking mathematics to the humanities can help to humanise mathematics, reaffirming its purposeful nature and showing how it is a social and cultural product that we should be proud to have developed. Connecting mathematical ideas to the performing arts can help pupils explore mathematical ideas in a more well-rounded way, and reconnect many mathematical concepts to the exploration and enquiry from which they originally emerged.

Of course, it is true that cross-curricular activity should be undertaken alongside other forms of practice, and there are many demands on a mathematics teacher; the learning of mathematics also places particular psychological demands on an individual, and these need to be planned for and addressed. However, there is little point building up pupils' mathematical technique and accuracy if they never have the chance to apply it; in some ways this is like learning the techniques and skills needed to pass a ball but never playing in a football match.

These are exciting times to be a teacher of mathematics. New qualifications and demands from industry have the potential to give rise to fresh opportunities for cross-curricular practice in a mathematics classroom. Developments in technology offer new possibilities for quantifying activity and gathering data. Outside of school new interdisciplinary fields are continuing to develop and emerge, containing exciting new ways in which mathematics comes alive. However, there is still a vast disconnect between the way in which mathematics is genuinely used in the world and the way in which it is perceived and presented in the secondary school classroom. Cross-curricular teaching and learning in mathematics is an important step towards bridging this gap. We have to remember ourselves that mathematics is an exciting and essential discipline and to remind other mathematics teachers of that fact. Ultimately, as teachers, we are charged with presenting our subject to our pupils in not only the best, but the most honest way possible. The ways in which you choose to accept this challenge, and the directions in which you might decide to develop your practice, are up to you.

Professional Standards for QTS

This chapter will help you meet the following Q standards: Q6, Q7, Q8, Q22, Q29.

Professional Standards for Teachers

This chapter will help you meet the following core standards: C6, C7, C8, C15, C26, C35.

Further reading

QCA (2009) *Engaging Mathematics for All Learners*.
This is an excellent publication which touches on many of the themes of this book. It contains a large number of ideas and case studies, many of which have a cross-curricular element, and also offers some further advice about how to make it all happen.

Bibliography

Ainley, J., Bills, L. and Wilson, K. (2005) 'Designing Spreadsheet-Based Tasks for Purposeful Algebra', *International Journal of Computers for Mathematical Learning*, 10(3): 191–215.

Albarn, K. (1991) 'Proportion: The Measure of Art', in Jones, L. (ed.), *Teaching Mathematics and Art*, Cheltenham: Stanley Thornes.

Alexander, R. (2008) *Towards Dialogic Teaching*: *Rethinking Classroom Talk*, fourth edition, Cambridge: Dialogos.

Ashcraft, M.H. and Ridley, K.S. (2005) 'Math Anxiety and Its Cognitive Consequences', in Campbell, J. (ed.), *Handbook of Mathematical Cognition*, Hove: Psychology Press.

Bassok, M. and Holyoak, K.J. (1993) 'Pragmatic Knowledge and Conceptual Structure: Determinants of Transfer Between Quantitative Domains', in Detterman, D.K. and Sternberg, R.J. (eds), *Transfer on Trial: Intelligence, Cognition and Instruction*, Norwood, NJ: Ablex

BBC News (2010) *Inflation accelerates to 3.5% in the UK*, online, available at: http://news.bbc.co.uk/1/hi/business/8517156.stm [accessed May 2010].

Beare, R. (1997) *Mathematics in Action: Modelling the Real World Using Mathematics*, Bromley: Richard Beare and Chartwell-Bratt.

Becta (2009) *ICT in Secondary Mathematics: A Pupil's Entitlement*, online, available at: http://schools.becta.org.uk/index.php?section=cu&catcode=ss_cu_ac_mat_03&rid=17339 [accessed May 2010].

Bell, E.T. (1951) *Mathematics: Queen and Servant of Science*, New York: McGraw-Hill.

Bell, M., Cordingly, P. and Goodchild, L. (2008) *Map of Research Reviews QCA Building the Evidence Base Project: September 2007–March 2011*, CUREE, online, available at: www.curee-paccts.com/resources/publications/map-research-reviews [accessed May 2010].

Black, P. and Atkin, J.M. (eds) (1996) *Changing the Subject: Innovations in Science, Mathematics and Technology Education*, London: Routledge for OECD.

——, Harrison, C., Lee, C., Marshall, B. and Wiliam, D. (2003) *Assessment for Learning: Putting it Into Practice*, Maidenhead: Open University Press.

Blastland, M. and Dilnot, A. (2008) *The Tiger That Isn't*, London: Profile.

Bloomfield, A. and Vertes, B. (2005) *People Maths: Hidden Depths*, Derby: Association of Teachers of Mathematics.

Blum, W., Galbraith, P.L., Henn, H.-W. and Niss, M. (eds) (2007) *Modelling and Applications in Mathematics Education: The 14th ICMI Study*, New York: Springer.

Boaler, J. (1994) 'When Do Girls Prefer Football to Fashion? An Analysis of Female Underachievement in Relation to 'Realistic' Mathematic Contexts', *British Educational Research Journal*, 20(5): 551–564.

Boyle, D. and Roddick, A. (2004) *Numbers*, Chichester: Anita Roddick Publications.

Britton, J. (2003) 'Escher in the Classroom', in Schattschneider, D. and Emmer, M. (eds), *M.C. Escher's Legacy: A Centennial Celebration*, New York: Springer.

Brodsky, L. (2008) 'The Use of Mathematics in KS3/KS4 Science Classes', *BSRLM Informal Proceedings*, 28(3): 7–12.

Brown, J.S., Collins, A. and Duguid, P. (1989) 'Situated Cognition and the Culture of Learning', *Educational Researcher*, 18(1): 32–42.

Brown, W.M., Cronk, L., Grochow, K., Jacobson, A., Liu, C.K., Popović, Z. and Trivers, R. (2005) 'Dance Reveals Symmetry Especially in Young Men', *Nature*, 438: 1148–1150.

Bruner, J. (1960) *The Process of Education*, Cambridge, MA: Harvard University Press.

—— (1966) *Towards a Theory of Instruction*, Cambridge, MA: Harvard University Press.

Catrambone, R. and Holyoak, K.J. (1990) 'Learning Subgoals and Methods for Solving Probability Problems', *Memory and Cognition*, 18(6): 593–603.

Coldea, R., Tennant, D.A., Wheeler, E.M., Wawrzynska, E., Prabhakaran, D., Telling, M., Habicht, K., Smeibidl, P. and Kiefer, K. (2010) 'Quantum Criticality in an Ising Chain: Experimental Evidence for Emergent E_8 Symmetry', *Science*, 327(5962): 177–180.

DATA (2008) *Cross-Curricular Links – Numeracy*, online, available at: www.data.org.uk/index. php?option=com_content&view=article&id=311&Itemid=372 [accessed May 2010].

Davis, P.J. (1994) 'Mathematics and Art: Cold Calipers Against Warm Flesh?', in Ernest, P. (ed.), *Mathematics, Education and Philosophy: An International Perspective*, London: Falmer Press.

—— and Hersh, R. (1983) *The Mathematical Experience*, Harmondsworth: Penguin.

Detterman, D.K. (1993) 'The Case for the Prosecution: Transfer as an Epiphenomenon', in Detterman, D.K. and Sternberg, R.J. (eds), *Transfer on Trial: Intelligence, Cognition and Instruction*, Norwood, NJ: Ablex

Dettori, G., Garuti, R. and Lemut, E. (2001) 'From Arithmetic to Algebraic Thinking by Using a Spreadsheet' in Sutherland, R., Rojano, T., Bell, A. and Lins, R. (eds), *Perspectives on School Algebra*, Dordrecht: Kluwer.

Devlin, K. and Lorden, G. (2007) *The Numbers Behind Numb3rs™*, London: Plume.

Dewdney, A.K. (1993) *200% of Nothing*, Chichester: John Wiley and Sons.

DfEE (2001) *Key Stage 3 National Strategy Framework for teaching mathematics: Years 7, 8 and 9*, London: DfEE.

DfEE/QCA (1999) *Mathematics: The National Curriculum for England, Key Stages 1-4*, London: DfEE/QCA.

DfES (2007) *Study Plus Handbook*, London: DfES, also online, available at: www.nationalstrategies. standards.dcsf.gov.uk/node/174545?uc=force_deep [accessed May 2010].

Dolton, P. and Vignoles, A. (2002) 'The Return on Post-Compulsory School Mathematics Study', *Economica*, 69(273): 113–141.

Dweck, C. (2000) *Self-theories: Their Role in Motivation, Personality and Development*, Lillington, NC: Psychology Press.

Eagle, M.R. (1995) *Exploring Mathematics through History*, Cambridge: Cambridge University Press.

Eastaway, R. and Wyndham, J. (2005) *Why do Buses Come in Threes? The Hidden Mathematics of Everyday Life*, new edition, London: Portico.

Edington, W.E. (1937) 'Vitalizing Mathematics', *National Mathematics Magazine*, 12(1): 27–38.

English, C. (1999) 'Modelling for the New Millennium' in Hoyles, C., Morgan, C. and Woodhouse, G. (eds), *Rethinking the Mathematics Curriculum*, London: Falmer Press.

Ernest, P. (1991) *The Philosophy of Mathematics Education*, London: Falmer.

Fauvel, J., Flood, R. and Wilson, R. (eds) (2003) *Music and Mathematics: From Pythagoras to Fractals*, Oxford: Oxford University Press.

Faux, G. and Hepburn, B. (2008) 'Quilting with Year 6', *Mathematics Teaching*, 210: 27–31, online, available at: www.atm.org.uk/journal/archive/mt210files/ATM-MT210-27-31.pdf.

Fox, D. (1983) 'Personal Theories of Teaching', *Studies in Higher Education*, 8(2): 151–163.

Frank, R.H. (2007) *The Economic Naturalist: Why Economics Explains Almost Everything*, London: Virgin Books.

French, D. (2002) *Teaching and Learning Algebra*, London: Continuum.

Freudenthal, H. (1991) *Revisiting Mathematics Education: China Lectures*, Kluwer, Dordrecht.

Gardner, H. (2006) *Multiple Intelligences: New Horizons*, New York: Basic Books.

Gardner, M. (1988) *Time Travel and Other Mathematical Bewilderments*, New York: W.H. Freeman.

Gattegno, C. (1970) *What We Owe Children: The Subordination of Teaching to Learning*, London: Routledge and Kegan Paul.

Graham, A. (2006) *Developing Thinking in Statistics*, London: Paul Chapman Publishing.

Hawkin, W. (1994) 'Art and Mathematics: A View From Art', *BSRLM Informal Proceedings*, 14(3): 38–45.

Heathcote, D. and Bolton, G. (1995) *Drama for Learning: Dorothy Heathcote's Mantle of the Expert Approach to Education*, Portsmouth, NH: Heinemann.

Henry, J. (2007) 'Professor Pans 'Learning Style' Teaching Method' *Telegraph* (online), 29 Jul 2007, online, available at: www.telegraph.co.uk/news/uknews/1558822/Professor-pans-learning-style-teaching-method.html [accessed May 2010].

Hiebert, J. and Lefevre, P. (1986) 'Conceptual and Procedural Knowledge in Mathematics: An Introductory Analysis', in Hiebert, J. (ed.), *Conceptual and Procedural Knowledge: The Case of Mathematics*, Mahwah, NJ: Lawrence Erlbaum Associates.

Hofstadter, D.R. (1986) *Metamagical Themas: Questing for the Essence of Mind and Pattern*, London: Penguin.

Howson, A.G. (1982) *A History of Mathematics Education in England*, Cambridge: Cambridge University Press.

Hoyles, C., Noss, R., Kent, P. and Bakker, A. (2010) *Improving Mathematics at Work: The Need for Techno-Mathematical Literacies*, London: Routledge.

Huff, D. (1954) *How to Lie with Statistics*, London: Gollancz.

Jäppinen, A.-K. (2005) 'Thinking and Content Learning of Mathematics and Science as Cognitional Development in Content and Integrated Language Learning (CLIL): Teaching Through a Foreign Language in Finland', *Language and Education*, 19(2): 148–169.

Johnston-Wilder, P. (2005) 'Thinking Statistically: Interactive Statistics' in Johnston-Wilder, S. and Pimm, D. (eds), *Teaching Secondary Mathematics with ICT*, Maidenhead: Open University Press.

Johnston-Wilder, S. and Lee, C. (2010) 'Mathematical resilience', *Mathematics Teaching*, 218: 38–41.

Johnston-Wilder, S. and Mason, J. (2005) *Developing Thinking in Geometry*, London: Paul Chapman Publishing.

Johnston-Wilder, S. and Pimm, D. (eds) (2005) *Teaching Secondary Mathematics with ICT*, Maidenhead: Open University Press.

Jones, K. and Edwards, R. (2010) 'Planning for Mathematics Learning' in Johnston-Wilder, S., Johnston-Wilder, P., Pimm, D. and Lee, C. (eds) *Learning to Teach Mathematics in the Secondary School: A Companion to School Experience*, third edition, London: Routledge.

Jones, L. (1991) 'Tessellations and the Work of M.C. Escher', in Jones, L. (ed.) *Teaching Mathematics and Art*, Cheltenham: Stanley Thornes.

Joseph, G.G. (1991) *The Crest of the Peacock: Non-European Roots of Mathematics*, London: I.B. Tauris.

Katz, V.J. (1998) *A History of Mathematics: An Introduction*, second edition, Harlow: Addison-Wesley.

Küchemann, D. (1981) 'Algebra', in Hart, K., Brown, M., Küchemann, D., Kerslake, D., Ruddock, G. and McCartney, M. (eds), *Children's Understanding of Mathematics: 11–16*, London: John Murray.

Lampbert, M. and Blunk, M.L. (eds) (1998) *Talking Mathematics in School: Studies of Teaching and Learning*, Cambridge: Cambridge University Press.

Lave, J. (1988) *Cognition in Practice*, Cambridge: Cambridge University Press.

learndirect (2008) *Brits Pay the Price for Poor Maths and English*, original research results, summary online, available at: www.ufi.com/home2/news/presscentre/release/release.asp?id=214 [accessed May 2010].

Lee, C. (2006) *Language for Learning Mathematics: Assessment for Learning in Practice*, Buckingham: Open University Press.

—— (2009) 'Fixed or Growth – Does It Matter?', *Mathematics Teaching*, 212: 44–46.

—— and Lawson, C. (1996) 'Numeracy through Literacy', *Educational Action Research*, 4(1): 59–72.

Levitin, D.J. (2007) *This is Your Brain on Music: Understanding a Human Obsession*, London: Atlantic Books.

MacKernan, J. (2000) 'Not for the Classroom', *Mathematics Teaching*, 172: 40–45.

Magnello, E. (2010) 'Florence Nightingale: A Victorian Statistician', *Mathematics in School*, 39(3): 20–21.

Mason, J. and Johnston-Wilder, S. (2006) *Designing and Using Mathematical Tasks*, St. Albans: Tarquin.

Mason, J., Graham, A. and Johnston-Wilder, S. (2005) *Developing Thinking in Algebra*, London: Paul Chapman Publishing.

MEI (2009) *QCA Consultation on Level 3 Mathematics: MEI Position Paper*, online, available at: www.mei.org.uk/files/pdf/MEI_A-level_position_statement_Final.pdf [accessed May 2010].

Metz, M. (1991) 'Islamic Design', in Jones, L. (ed.), *Teaching Mathematics and Art*, Cheltenham: Stanley Thornes.

Middleton, J.A. and Spanias, P.A. (1999) 'Motivation for Achievement in Mathematics: Findings, Generalizations, and Criticisms of the Research', *Journal for Research in Mathematics Education*, 30(1): 65–88.

Millennium Project (2009) *Global Challenges for Humanity*, online, available at: www.millennium-project.org/millennium/challenges.html [accessed May 2010].

Morgan, C. (1998) *Writing Mathematically: The Discourse of Investigation*, London: Falmer.

—— (2001) 'The Place of Pupil Writing in Learning, Teaching and Assessing Mathematics' in Gates, P. (ed.), *Issues in Mathematics Teaching*, London: RoutledgeFalmer.

Munz, P., Hudea, I., Imad, J. and Smith? [sic], R.J. (2009) 'When Zombies Attack!: Mathematical Modelling of an Outbreak of Zombie Infection' in Tchuenche, J.M. and Chiyaka, C. (eds), *Infectious Disease Modelling Research Progress*, New York: Nova Science, also online, available at: www.mathstat.uottawa.ca/~rsmith/Zombies.pdf [accessed May 2010].

Musto, G. (2009) 'Pythagoras' Canvas', *Mathematics Teaching*, 213: 26–29.

Nardi, E. and Steward, S. (2003) 'Is Maths T.I.R.E.D.? A Profile of Quiet Disaffection in the Secondary Maths Classroom', *British Educational Research Journal*, 29(3): 345–367.

NCETM (2008) *Mathematics Matters: Final Report*, London: NCETM Publications, also online, available at: www.ncetm.org.uk/files/309231/Mathematics+Matters+Final+Report.pdf [accessed May 2010].

Noyes, A. (2007) *Rethinking School Mathematics*, London: Paul Chapman Publishing.

Nunes, T., Schliemann, A.D. and Carraher, D.W. (1993) *Street Mathematics and School Mathematics*, Cambridge: Cambridge University Press.

Ofsted (2009) *Mathematics: Understanding the Score – Improving Practice in Mathematics Teaching at Secondary Level*, London: Ofsted Publications, also online, available at: www.ofsted.gov.uk/Ofsted-home/Publications-and-research/Browse-all-by/Documents-by-type/Thematic-reports/Mathematics-understanding-the-score-Improving-practice-in-mathematics-secondary [accessed May 2010].

Oldknow, A. and Taylor, R. (2003) *Teaching Mathematics Using ICT*, London: Continuum.

Onion, A., Lane, P., Lister, A. and Wintle, K. (2008) 'Bowland Maths: Problem Solving in Key Stage 3', *Mathematics Teaching*, 210: 20–26.

Papert, S. (1991) 'Situating Constructionism', in Harel, I. and Papert, S. (eds), *Constructionism: Research Reports and Essays, 1985–1990*, Norwood, NJ: Ablex.

—— (1993) *Mindstorms: Children, Computers and Powerful Ideas*, London: Harvester Wheatsheaf.

Parsons, S. and Bynner, J. (2006) *Does Numeracy Matter More?*, London: NRDC.

Piaget, J. (1970) *Genetic Epistemology*, New York: Columbia University Press.

—— and Inhelder, B. (1956) *The Child's Conception of Space*, London: Routledge and Kegan Paul.

Picker, S.H. and Berry, J.S. (2000) 'Investigating Pupils' Images of Mathematicians', *Educational Studies in Mathematics*, 43(1): 65–94.

Pohl, R.F. (ed.) (2004) *Cognitive Illusions: A Handbook on Fallacies and Biases in Thinking, Judgement and Memory*, Hove: Psychology Press.

Polster, B. (2003) *The Mathematics of Juggling*, London: Springer.

QCA (2007) *The National Curriculum 2007: Statutory Requirements for Key Stages 3 and 4*, London: QCA, extended version with additional guidance online, available at: http://curriculum. qcda.gov.uk/key-stages-3-and-4/index.aspx [accessed May 2010].

—— (2009) *Engaging Mathematics for All Learners*, London: QCA, also online, available at: http://orderline.qcda.gov.uk/gempdf/184721942X.PDF [accessed May 2010].

QCDA (2010) *The National Curriculum Primary Handbook*, London: QCDA.

Ransom, P. (1999) *Cross-Curricular Work Involving Mathematics Using Hand-Held Technology*, online, available at: www.standards.dfes.gov.uk/ntrp/lib/pdf/handheld.pdf [accessed May 2010].

Ransom, P. and Shiers, M. (2010) 'Yo ho ho-Ratio: Some Mathematics of Trafalgar or How Lord Nelson Inspired Curriculum Development in Mathematics', *Mathematics in School*, 39(3): 24–28.

Reed, S.K., Dempster, A. and Ettinger, M. (1985) 'Usefulness of Analogous Solutions for Solving Algebra Word problems', *Journal of Experimental Psychology: Learning, Memory and Cognition*, 11(1): 106–125.

Richardson, F.C. and Suinn, R.M. (1972) 'The Mathematics Anxiety Rating Scale: Psychometric Data', *Journal of Counseling Psychology*, 19(6): 551–554.

Rittle-Johnson, B. and Alibabi, M.W. (1999) 'Conceptual and Procedural Knowledge of Mathematics: Does One Lead to the Other?', *Journal of Educational Psychology*, 91(1): 175–189.

Robson, E. (2002) 'Words and Pictures: New Light on Plimpton 322', *The American Mathematical Monthly*, 109(2): 105–120.

Rogers, L. (2010) 'Golden Rules for Studying the History of Mathematics', *Mathematics in School*, 39(3): 5.

Rojano, T. (1996) 'Problem Solving in a Spreadsheet Environment' in Bednarz, N., Kieran, C. and Lee, L. (eds), *Approaches to Algebra – Perspectives for Research and Teaching*, Dordrecht: Kluwer.

RSA (2008) *Opening Minds*, online, available at: www.thersa.org/projects/opening-minds [accessed July 2010].

Savage, J. (2011) *Cross-Curricular Teaching and Learning in the Secondary School*, Abingdon: Routledge.

Seikkula-Leino, J. (2007) 'CLIL Learning: Achievement Levels and Affective Factors', *Language and Education*, 21(4): 328–341.

Shennan, S. (1983) 'Disentangling Data' in Howson, G. and McLone, R. (eds), *Maths at Work*, London: Heinemann Educational Books.

Singh, S. (2000) *The Code Book: The Secret History of Codes and Code Breaking*, London: Fourth Estate.

Skemp, R.R. (1976) 'Instrumental Understanding and Relational Understanding', *Mathematics Teaching*, 77: 20–26.

—— (1986) *The Psychology of Learning Mathematics*, second edition, Harmondsworth: Penguin.

Stager, G.S. (2002) 'Computationally-Rich Constructionism and At-Risk Learners', in McDougall, A., Murnane, J. and Chambers, D. (eds), *Proc. WCCE2001 Australian Topics: Selected Papers from the Seventh World Conference on Computers in Education*, Copehagen, Denmark: ACS. CRPIT 8: 105–111, online, available at: www.crpit.com/confpapers/ CRPITV8Stager.pdf [accessed May 2010].

Tall, D.O. (ed.) (1991) *Advanced Mathematical Thinking*, London: Kluwer Academic.

Thorndike, E.L. (1922) *The Psychology of Arithmetic*, New York: Macmillan.

—— (1923) *The Psychology of Algebra*, New York: Macmillan.

Toumasis, C. (2004) 'A mathematical diet model', *Teaching Mathematics and its Applications*, 23(4): 165–171.

Tversky, A. and Kahneman, D. (1982) 'Judgements of and by Representativeness', in Kahneman, D., Slovic, P. and Tversky, A. (eds), *Judgement Under Uncertainty: Heuristics and Biases*, Cambridge: Cambridge University Press.

Tytherleigh, B. and Watson, A. (1987) 'Mathematics and Dance', *Mathematics Teaching*, 121: 39–43.

von Glasersfeld, E. (1995) *Radical Constructivism: A Way of Knowing and Learning*, London: Falmer Press.

Waks, S. (1988) 'Mathematics and Electronics: The Conceptual Transfer Problem', *Physics Education*, 23(4): 234–238.

Ward-Penny, R. (2008) 'The Performing Arts in the Mathematics Classroom', *Mathematics in School*, 37(4): 37.

—— 'Context or Con? How Might We Better Represent The 'Real-World' in the Classroom?', *Mathematics in School*, 39(1): 10–12.

—— and the University of Warwick Secondary Mathematics PGCE Students (2010) 'Mathematical Haikus', *Mathematics in School*, 39(4): 9.

Watson, A. (1999) 'Working on Wonder and Wondering: Making Sense of the Spiritual in Mathematics Teaching', *Mathematics Education Review*, 11: 30–40.

—— (2004) 'Dance and Mathematics: Power of Novelty in the Teaching of Mathematics', Paper from Topic Study Group at ICME 10, online, available at: www.icme-organisers. dk/tsg14/TSG14-11.pdf [accessed May 2010].

Weiss, H. and Weiss, V. (2003) 'The Golden Mean as Clock Cycle of Brain Waves', *Chaos, Solitons and Fractals*, 18(4): 643–652.

Wellington, J. and Ireson, G. (2008) *Science Learning, Science Teaching*, Abingdon: Routledge.

Whitcombe, A. and Donaldson, M. (1988) 'Shongo Networks: A Multicultural Theme for the Classroom', *Mathematics in School*, 17(5): 34–38.

Wigner, E. (1960) 'The Unreasonable Effectiveness of Mathematics in the Natural Sciences', *Communications in Pure and Applied Mathematics*, 13(1): 1–14.

Zakaria, N. (2004) 'A Study of the Nature of Knowledge Transfer Across Subject Boundaries: Comparing Procedural Students and Conceptual Students at University Level', unpublished PhD thesis, University of Warwick.

Index